Utopianism

Concepts in Social Thought

Series Editor: Frank Parkin

Published Titles

Concepts in Social Thought

Utopianism

Krishan Kumar

University of Minnesota Press

Minneapolis

Published by the University of Minnesota Press
2037 University Avenue Southeast, Minneapolis MN 55414

Printed in Great Britain

Library of Congress Cataloging-in-Publication Data

Kumar, Krishan.
    Utopianism/Krishan Kumar.
        p.   cm. – (Concepts in social thought)
    Includes bibliographical references and index.
    ISBN 0–8166–1974–3 (HC)   ISBN 0–8166–1975–1 (PB)
    1. Utopias – History.   I. Title.   II. Series.
HX806.K863   1991
335′.02′09 – dc20
                                             90–19964
                                              CIP

Contents

To John and Dymphna

Preface

A short book of this kind cannot hope to do full justice to so complex and many-sided a subject as utopia. I have tried to indicate something of the variety of the concept, a variety stemming largely from the fact that utopia has a history. At the same time I did not want to leave the impression of too diffuse a treatment. So I have also tried to argue a particular case about utopia: about its origins, its development and its uses as a type of social theory. In doing so I hope to have brought out its distinctiveness as a literary form put to the service of social analysis and social criticism. That distinctiveness has sometimes led to its downgrading in the eyes of social theorists. Utopia is regarded as an agreeable but eccentric by-way leading off the broad highway of Western social thought. I have tried to suggest rather that utopia deals with many of the same issues as more conventional social theory, but in its own way. That way is all the more effective for looking at familiar problems from an unfamiliar angle, and in a different light.

Utopia has been in and out of fashion at various times in its 500-year existence; but it has shown remarkable resilience as a form and as a way of thinking. A temporary eclipse does not amount to extinction. The familiar pronouncements about the 'death of utopia' today ignore not just this but also the many uses to which utopia has been put. Utopia is a variegated project, the meeting place of many purposes and many disciplines of thought. The richness of its resources gives it a great capacity for survival, and revival. As we approach the end of the second millennium we shall see that there is much for it to do (as I indicate in my last chapter).

I should like to thank Frank Parkin for inviting me to contribute to the series; and Ray Cunningham for his forbearance in the face of too many deadlines not met. I am grateful to them both for their encouragement and support.

Krishan Kumar
Canterbury, Kent

The Elements of Utopia

Dreams and realities

Utopia is nowhere (*outopia*) and it is also somewhere good (*eutopia*). To live in a world that cannot be but where one fervently wishes to be: that is the literal essence of utopia. To this extent utopia does share the quality of a dream. To deny that would be to miss one of the most powerful sources of its appeal. But were that all it was, were utopia no more than a waking dream, we would have no more than a passing interest in it.

The land of Utopia was discovered by Sir Thomas More in 1516, in his book that first named and described it.[1] Here was a place, imaginary, it was true, and accordingly futile to seek out, that nevertheless existed tantalizingly on the edge of possibility, somewhere just beyond the boundary of the real. More went out of his way to assist this feeling. His traveller-narrator, Raphael Hythloday, had supposedly accompanied Amerigo Vespucci on his expeditions in the wake of Columbus's recent discovery of the New World. Remaining in the New World after Vespucci's fourth expedition, Hythloday continued his travels on his own and came upon the island of Utopia. Utopia was therefore no more than an extra voyage's distance away from the American lands already described with such excitement by every returning mariner. It was on the edge of the known world – and the known world was expanding daily. Moreover, many of the customs of Utopia as described by Hythloday – its communism, absence of monarchy, scorn of gold and jewels – could be found in Vespucci's own account – 'now in print and abroad in every man's hands'[2] – of his encounters with the peoples of the New World.

More's jesting fable (Hythloday = 'a distributor of nonsense') nicely maintains the ambivalence of the utopian project throughout. The description of Utopian customs and institutions that occupies Part 2 of his book has the irony and playfulness that characterized many of the products of the Renaissance humanists. Part 1, however, the searing indictment of Tudor England, is in deadly earnest. The second part was written before the first. It was only after sketching the picture of Utopia that More seems to have seen the opportunity – or the need – for delivering at the same time a lecture on contemporary English vices. Utopia is clearly meant to hold the mirror up to More's England. Here is a pagan society which, even though it lacks the inestimable benefits of Christianity, has nevertheless managed to achieve a state of near perfection.

But did More seriously think that England – or any other country – could become Utopia? Did *Utopia* present 'a program of social reform' – on behalf, say, of the London merchants? Can one say of it that 'in every detail [it] had a practical meaning in More's day'?[3] And was that practical meaning – following another interpretation – along the lines, 'You Europeans call yourselves Christians, but the Utopians show what a truly Christian life should be. They, not you, are the real Christians. Imitate them'? Or was *Utopia* in no way intended as a programmatic statement, but more in the nature of a *jeu d'esprit*, a humanist tract written for the delight and edification of More's scholarly friends such as Erasmus and Peter Giles?[4] More covered his tracks so cleverly that we shall never know for certain. At the end of *Utopia* he says: 'I must needs confess and grant that many things be in the Utopian weal-public which in our cities I may rather wish for than hope for.'[5] This seems to leave Utopia in the realm of the dream or wish-fulfilling fantasy. At the same time there is much in Utopian values and customs that clearly relate to More's practical preoccupations as a lawyer, humanist reformer and statesman.

So from its very inception with More utopia embodies two impulses, tending often in opposite directions. It is more than a social or political tract aiming at reform, however comprehensive. It always goes beyond the immediately practicable, and it may go so far beyond as to be in most realistic senses wholly impracticable. But it is never simple dreaming. It always has one foot in reality. H. G. Wells's statement of his intent in *A Modern Utopia*

(1905) neatly captures this tension between possibility and practicability.

> Our business here is to be Utopian, to make vivid and credible if we can, first this facet and then that, of an imaginary whole and happy world. Our deliberate intention is to be not, indeed, impossible, but most distinctly impracticable, by every scale that reaches only between today and tomorrow.[6]

Utopia's value lies not in its relation to present practice but in its relation to a possible future. Its 'practical' use is to overstep the immediate reality to depict a condition whose clear desirability draws us on, like a magnet. Here the very visionary and 'impracticable' quality of utopia is its strength. Just as the hidden God, who will always remain hidden, provokes us to try to uncover the veil, to discover perfect truth and perfect morality, so utopia's 'nowhereness' incites the search for it. A boundary can either confine and inhibit or it can invite us to go beyond. The commonly accepted boundary of the possible is always contingent, always dependent on the particular circumstances of time and place. Utopia breaks through that boundary. It attempts to lift the veil both for its own time and, conceivably, for all time. Utopia describes a state of impossible perfection which nevertheless is in some genuine sense not beyond the reach of humanity. It is here if not now.

All this suggests that utopia, too, has its boundaries. It is not just any dream of impossible perfection. It is a way of looking at the world that has its own history and character. This does not mean that the utopian form is sharply defined. Quite the opposite, in fact. Having a history means being an entity that changes. But these changes are not random. They occur within a tradition that sets certain limits to what utopia can do. Utopia may be nowhere but, historically and conceptually, it cannot be just *anywhere*.

What are the boundaries of utopia? What are its features as a 'structure of thought'?[7] There have been many varieties of the ideal society or the ideal condition of humanity. We need to consider some of these briefly before we can see what is distinctive about the utopian variety.

The Golden Age, Arcadia, Paradise

Virtually all societies have some myth or memory of a Golden Age, a time of beginnings in which humanity lived in a state of perfect happiness and fulfilment. Most frequently this myth takes a primitivist form. The 'original' time or condition was one of simplicity and sufficiency. There was an instinctive harmony between man and nature. Men's needs were few and their desires limited. Both were easily satisfied by the abundance of nature. Hence there were no motives for war or oppression. Nor, for the same reason, was there any need to toil painfully for long hours. In the Golden Age men and women lived in a state of ease, plenty, and freedom. Simple and pious, they were and felt themselves close to the gods.

For the West, the myth of the Golden Age was definitively expounded by Hesiod, Plato, Virgil and Ovid. Virgil's Arcadia, a region in the Peloponnese of rustic contentment, provided the stuff of the literary pastoral until the end of the eighteenth century. Two highly influential treatments of this were Montaigne's essay in praise of primitive simplicity, 'Of Cannibals' (1580), and Sir Philip Sidney's prose romance *The Arcadia* (1590).

The passages from the Greek and Roman poets are well known.[8] As an indication of the worldwide prevalence of the myth of the Golden Age, here is the account of the *Krita Yuga*, the First and Perfect Age, from the Hindu epic, the *Mahabharata*:

> The Krita Yuga was so named because there was but one religion, and all men were saintly: therefore they were not required to perform religious ceremonies. Holiness never grew less, and the people did not decrease. There were no gods in the Krita Yuga, and there were no demons . . . Men neither bought nor sold; there were no poor and no rich; there was no need to labour, because all that men required was obtained by the power of will; the chief virtue was the abandonment of all worldly desires. The Krita Yuga was without disease; there was no lessening with the years; there was no hatred or vanity, or evil thought whatsoever; no sorrow, no fear. All mankind could attain to supreme blessedness.[9]

Other accounts of the Golden Age are the Dreamtime of the Australian Aborigines and the Chinese Taoist Age of Perfect Virtue. In the West there was also the fusion of the pagan Golden Age with the Judaeo-Christian Paradise. Most intensely in the drawings and paintings of Dürer, Bosch and the Cranach family, the Biblical story of Adam and Eve in the Garden of Eden was superimposed on the classical description of the Golden Age. Other celebrated pictures of Paradise were to be found in Dante's *The Divine Comedy* (c.1321) and Milton's *Paradise Lost* (1667).

The Paradise myth did not, however, simply echo the view of an original Golden Age. The Christian Paradise lay not only in the past but also in the future. Paradise, once lost, could and would be regained. In John Bunyan's *The Pilgrim's Progress from This World to That Which Is to Come* (1684) the hero Christian overcomes all earthly obstacles to reach his goal – the Celestial City, a Heavenly Paradise that restores the glory of the world before the Fall. In Dostoyevsky's story, 'The Dream of a Queer Fellow' (1877), the protagonist introduces corruption and brings about a Fall from Paradise; but he seeks to restore it by preaching forgiveness and brotherly love.

The Christian Paradise was by no means alone in its anticipation of redemption and renewal. Other cultures also saw a time of floods, cataclysms and human misery being eventually succeeded by the return of the Golden Age, the original Creation-Time.[10] No more was Christianity alone in its belief – strong until the sixteenth century – that the lost Garden of Eden still physically existed somewhere on earth. Earthly Paradises abound in the legends of many cultures.[11] The Greeks and Romans of antiquity had their Islands of the Blessed, to which were translated the living bodies of heroes who lived upon them a life free from care and full of noble pleasure. The Tibetans preserved the legend of Shambhala, a mystical kingdom in a remote valley in the Himalayas. Here perfect enlightenment and pure Buddhism ruled.

Christianity largely built upon ancient legends of terrestrial Paradises. The Kingdom of Prester John combined the pagan Fortunate Isles with the Biblical Eden. St Brendan's Isle echoed a long-standing Celtic tradition that there existed a Paradise in the Western Ocean, the Atlantic. The legend of the seven Christian bishops who, fleeing Moorish Spain, discovered the beautiful island of Antilia in the Atlantic, was also based on earlier Atlantic myths. Christopher Columbus followed directly in this tradition in his belief that he had found the Garden of Eden when first he encountered the New World and its peoples. The New World in its turn renewed the Paradise myth, mixed in now with millennial themes.

The Land of Cockaygne

This has been aptly called the 'poor man's heaven'. It is the popular
counterpart to the poet's and priest's Golden Age and Paradise,
with their rather fastidious devotion to simplicity and spirituality.
Cockaygne, by contrast, is a land of extravagance, exuberance and
excess. It evokes words like Falstaffian and Gargantuan. Its master
themes are abundance and freedom from work. Everything is free
and available for the asking. Cooked larks fly straight into one's
mouth; the rivers run with wine; the more one sleeps, the more one
earns; sexual promiscuity is the norm; there is a fountain of youth
which keeps everyone young and active.

A famous mediaeval poem, actually an attack on sloth and
gluttony, vividly describes the Land of Cockagyne, 'out to sea, far
west of Spain'.[12] Here again the Christian rendering reflects older
classical accounts, especially as found in the Attic comedy and
Lucian's *True History*. In the literary Cockaygne, both in the
Christian and classical versions, the satirical intent is clear. It
remains so in the celebrated painting by Brueghel the Elder, in
which the roofs of the city are made of cake and citizens lie back
contentedly while gorgeous morsels of food drop straight into their
mouths. But from its earliest representations the poor man's heaven
became detached from its literary moorings and achieved independent status as a popular fantasy of pure hedonism: a cockney
paradise. It turns up in various forms in many times and places – as
Lubberland, Venusberg, Schlaraffenland, the Country of the
Young. Two of the best known versions, where the element of wish
fulfilment is at its clearest, are the American ballads *The Big Rock
Candy Mountains* and *Poor Man's Heaven*. Various festivals, such
as the Roman Saturnalia and the mediaeval Feast of Fools, both
characterized by popular licence and uninhibited indulgence, also
seem naturally to belong to the Cockaygne tradition.

The millennium

The millennium in its aspect as an ideal condition of humanity,
connects with the idea of 'the once and future Paradise'. It is both
Golden Age and New Era; primitive Paradise and Promised Land.
Both the beliefs and the movements associated with them oscillate

constantly between the two poles, lending to millenarianism equally the characteristics of extreme conservatism and extreme radicalism.

Millenarians believe that the end of this world, and of historical time, is at hand. A new world, and a new time, will be inaugurated, usually through the agency of a messiah: a saviour or deliverer. There will be many tribulations and mighty conflicts. The forces of evil will gather themselves up in a last bid for victory. But the good will triumph. The new era – the millennium – will be a time of peace, plenty and righteousness.

The millennium is both restitutive and retributive. It reverses the period of evil and suffering, and it rewards the virtuous for their fortitude while punishing evil-doers. But it is in its forward-looking character that the millennium most clearly distinguishes itself from the Golden Age and Paradise (notwithstanding the fact that these, too, in many versions are expected to recur). The millennium faces the future more than it harks back to the past. It works with an epochal scheme in which universal history is divided into stages leading inexorably to a final consummation in the millennium (itself a prologue to a Last Judgement and a final separation of saints and sinners). Of all ideal society conceptions, it is the millennium which most forcibly introduces the elements of time, process and history. The millennial Good Time restores something of the glory of the Golden Age, but it is also at the End of Time. It is a prelude to something radically new, something not experienced even in the original Paradise. It represents and at the same time reveals the completion of God's purpose in relation to man. The peculiar power of the millennial idea comes from the fact that in it eschatology complements futurology.

In Western thought Christian millenarianism continues Jewish messianism. The Jewish messiah was at first simply 'the anointed one', the king whose reign was consecrated by a rite of anointment with oil.[13] Later, following the destruction of the First Temple and the Babylonian exile, the term came to be applied to the future king, a descendant of the house of David, who would restore the Kingdom of Israel and bring about peace and happiness. This conception was linked to contemporary prophecies, such as those contained in *Isaiah*, of the appearance of a future ideal king (although the prophets themselves do not use the word messiah in this context).

As the miseries of the Jews piled up – persecution under the

Seleucid kings of Syria, submission to Rome, the destruction of Jerusalem and the Second Temple – messianism took on an increasingly apocalyptic flavour, as evidenced in the *Book of Daniel*. The messiah occasionally came to be seen in spiritualized, even transcendental, terms, as a more or less divine figure. But essentially Jewish messianism remained – at least in the ancient world – secular. Its character was fundamentally national, historical and political. The Golden Age that was to come would be here, on earth, under an earthly ruler. The Jews would be delivered from exile and restored to the Holy Land (Canaan) by a royal 'son of David'. Jerusalem would be rebuilt, the Temple reconstructed and reconsecrated. The Jews would live in peace and goodness under the rule of the Torah, the divinely given moral ordinance. In their daily liturgy, in the grace recited after every meal, in the prayers on Sabbath and holy days, Jews constantly reaffirmed these concrete features of their messianic belief.

Universalized and spiritualized, the concrete, this-worldly character of Jewish messianism lived on in Christian millenarianism, although often in devious and subterranean forms.[14] The Jewish Apocalyptic had already extended the messianic concept into the realms of the cosmic and the divine, and clothed it with eschatological significance. The coming of the messiah would herald the End of Days, the Day of Judgement, the resurrection of the dead, and the establishment of the heavenly kingdom. The theme of 'a new heaven and a new earth', central to the key Christian millenarian text, *The Revelation of St John the Divine*, was thus clearly prefigured in Jewish thought. So too, though less clearly, was the tendency to see the messiah not simply as 'the anointed one' but as 'the Lord's anointed'.

What Christianity added was a new sense of urgency, coupled with the explosive idea of a millennial Second Coming. This admittedly was frowned on from an early date as a heresy. The official Christian church, following Augustine, continued to insist that the new dispensation had already begun, with Christ's appearance among men, and that the Second Coming would spell the end of all earthly history. Christ would not come into the world a second time to establish some earthly kingdom lasting a thousand years. He would come to end the world and to pass a Final Judgement on all humankind. Thereafter there would be no earthly existence but only Heaven and Hell.

But although millenarianism was pronounced a heresy by the Council of Ephesus in AD 431 there never was any possibility that it would be stilled. The vision of a thousand-year period of bliss for the faithful, to be enjoyed here on earth, exerted an irresistible power. Throughout the centuries, right up to and including the twentieth century, millenarianism continued to inspire movements and ideas. The primary belief was taken from the *Book of Revelation*. Following a cataclysmic period of strife, and the emergence and defeat of the Antichrist, Christ would return and rule with his resurrected saints for a thousand years – a millennium – on earth. The precise character of that millennium was obscure in *Revelation*, except for the obvious point that it would be a period of surpassing virtue and happiness. Later commentators eked out the account with passages from Isaiah, Daniel, and Enoch. There were also unending disputes, fruitfully fuelled by the cryptic and oracular nature of the Apocalypse, as to whether the battle with the Antichrist would take place before or after the Second Coming; and whether Jesus's Second Coming would precede the millennium (premillennialism) or follow it (postmillennialism). These differences naturally had important effects on the disposition of believers. But what united them, what gave millenarianism its tremendous power, was the central belief that there would be a heaven on earth. The millennium would be a foretaste, the more delightful for being fleeting, of that eternal bliss which the faithful would enjoy in the everlasting life at the right hand of God.

Seen simply as a vision of an ideal condition of humanity, the millennium adds little to – is indeed somewhat sparser than – older notions of the Golden Age or Paradise. The picture of life in the millennial era is almost wilfully obscure (as obscure as life in the socialist utopia, and probably for the same reasons). What has made the millennium infinitely more powerful than the Golden Age or Paradise myths are the activities of the sects and movements that it has inspired. To a vision of perfection the millennium has added a dynamic dimension – an account of how it will be achieved – and the sense of an ordered or preordained history with a beginning, a middle and an end. All this has encouraged action. The belief in the certainty of earthly salvation has transformed behaviour, often on a revolutionary scale.

Millenarianism, despite the central role played by a messiah, is fundamentally a collectivist doctrine. It tells of a life to be enjoyed by the faithful as a group, as a community of saints. It also says that, sooner or later, that life will come. Such a belief has set in motion through the ages hundreds of sects convinced that the millennium had either already arrived or was imminent. Some took it upon themselves to be the midwives of the coming dispensation, their activities frequently bringing them into conflict with the authorities of the unregenerate world. Others quietly withdrew to live the pure life of the millennium, in the belief that it was already upon them and that Christ had returned to earth. In either case they attempted to live out their own vision of the millennial life, radically overturning the beliefs and practices of the surrounding society. In doing so they offered a model of the good life. Millenarians did not simply envisage or dream about the ideal society, a lost or future Golden Age; they lived it and so expressed the hope and the possibility that the whole world would live as they, in their transfigured state, were able to live.

In 1947 the discovery of the Dead Sea scrolls revealed the existence of a Jewish community, the Qumran community of the order of the Essenes, which from about 130 BC to AD 70 lived a life of exemplary piety in preparation for the Day of Judgement and the end of the world. For latter-day millenarians the life of the Qumran community – communal, monastic, ascetic – has provided something of a model; the more so perhaps as the existence of the community seems to have been contemporaneous with the writing of the *Book of Revelation*. Millenarianism has also been abundantly fed by the thought and practice of a host of other sects and movements: among them the communistic Taborites of fifteenth-century Bohemia, Thomas Muntzer's peasant followers and the Anabaptists of Munster in sixteenth-century Germany, the Diggers and Fifth Monarchists of the seventeenth-century English Civil War, the Shakers and Mormons of nineteenth-century America, and the Jehovah's Witnesses and Seventh Day Adventists (the former Millerites) of the twentieth century. Varied as these were and are, they are among the most arresting real-life examples of concerted action to bring in the millennial New Age; they have been, in different ways, models of the good life.

Millenarianism also proved remarkably adaptable in the face of changing cosmologies. With God dethroned and science and reason elevated in his place, millenarianism often took on secular form without giving up its basic constituents. Science and revolution were the new messiahs. The eighteenth -century philosophers aspired to create a 'heavenly city' by the light of Newtonian science; the French Revolution seemed to many to be ushering in the millennial reign of reason. Nineteenth-century social philosophers, too, often appeared to be merely rehearsing the scheme of the most influential millennial thinker, the twelfth-century Calabrian monk, Joachim of Fiore. Joachim's doctrine of the Three Ages, culminating in the love, peace and freedom of the Age of the Holy Spirit, seemed to find a direct echo in the philosophies of history of Saint-Simon, Hegel and Marx. Saint-Simon's scientific society, Hegel's age of the actualized Spirit, and Marx's society of full communism all carried strong millennial overtones. (So too, in a grotesque parody of Three Ages philosophy, did Hitler's Third Reich.)

It was the Christian millennium that named this particular variety of ideal-society thinking; and it was Christian millenarianism that stimulated the largest number of movements. Often this was in conditions of culture contact, as in the case of the Melanesian cargo cults, where Christian millennialism was grafted onto tribal beliefs. There was also the powerful development of Islamic millenarianism, where the Judaeo-Christian messiah reappeared as the Mahdi, 'the God-guided one' (occasionally fused with the equally messianic twelfth or 'hidden' imam in Shi´i Islam).[15]

But millenarianism, or something very much like it, has also been found without the Christian influence. Such seems to be the case with movements among the Guarani Indians of Brazil, the Karen of Burma, and the Indians of the Pacific North-West. The most powerful current of non-Christian millenarianism is, however, to be found in China. Taoism and Buddhism both contributed the idea of a messianic deliverance following a cataclysmic period of floods and epidemics, and leading to an era of peace and joy. Indigenous Chinese beliefs fused with imported Christian influences in the nineteenth century to produce the grandest millenarian movement in Chinese history, the Taiping Rebellion: a movement to create 'the heavenly kingdom of Great Peace and Equality'.[16]

The ideal city

If Christianity's principal – although by no means sole – contribution to ideal-society thinking was the millennium, that of ancient pagan thought was the ideal city. Ancient conceptions of the good life or the perfect commonwealth were firmly anchored to the form of the city. Lewis Mumford has gone so far as to claim that 'the first utopia was the city itself'. Hellenic reflection on the ideal city, he suggests, echoed 'the archetypal ancient city' as actually found in the ancient Near East. The ancient city was pre-eminently a work of art, or artifice; it was usually consecrated to a god, and thought of as his abode; it was ruled by a divinely ordained king; and its function was not so much the reproduction of daily material life as the cultivation and regulation of the sacred realm linking man to the cosmos. In this conception, 'the city itself was transmogrified into an ideal form – a glimpse of eternal order, a visible heaven on earth, a seat of life abundant – in other words, utopia'.[17]

The ideal city is the philosopher's contribution to utopia. Poets might picture Paradise and the Golden Age, devotees work for the millennium; the philosophers invented the ideal city as the earthly embodiment of the cosmic order which they deduced from first principles. The ideal city was the microcosmic reflection of the divinely regulated macrocosmic order. In its buildings, laws and social institutions it attempted to reproduce the harmony of the heavens. All ideal cities aspired to be a City of the Sun, as Campanella called his utopia; or, as Christians saw it following Augustine, the ideal earthly city should be a simulacrum of the City of God.

In that sense, as a representation of the cosmos, the city was 'natural'. It was the natural form at least for man, Aristotle claimed; the only place where he could lead the good life. The brutes and the gods had their own specific ways of mirroring the order of the cosmos. But in a more important sense the city was artificial. It was a construct, an artefact. The city was a creation of reason; and though reason was man's natural prerogative, his defining essence, it was an attribute needed as much in the correction of errors as in freely and spontaneously expressing man's nature. The city belonged to the divine order and must obey its principles; but the discovery and application of these principles were the work of human reflection and human action. The city, and only the city, offered the opportunity for the good life, but it was an opportunity more frequently lost than seized. The city was only potentially the site of the good life. Reason was necessary in its conception and construction; reason was also necessary in its guidance to prevent its lapse into corruption and decay. Rational planning, rational regulation and rational administration were essential to the good order of the city. Whether or not philosophers actually ruled, philosophic understanding was critical in the making and maintenance of the ideal city. Hence the characteristic features of the ideal city. These include first of all a recognition of the key role of the founders of cities and framers of constitutions: those who gave the law and made the rational order of the city. We encounter frequently in the classical world, as part myth, part history, the legendary founders Solon of Athens and Lycurgus of Sparta. These were further idealized by Plutarch in his *Lives*, where he makes of Solon and Lycurgus the virtual creators of (sharply contrasting) utopian societies. The *Lives* were popular in the Renaissance and Solon and Lycurgus became the prototypes of the founders and lawgivers of Renaissance utopias: King Utopus in More's *Utopia*, Sol in Campanella's *City of the Sun*, King Solamona in Bacon's *New Atlantis*.

The ideal city is systematically organized. It is a rational entity in a Weberian sense. Though there is room for private activities these take place within a strong framework of public management and control. This again reflects the communal, originally religious, purpose of the city. For the same reason there is often an elaborate social hierarchy. The divine hierarchy of the cosmos is mirrored in a functional specialization of tasks. So in Plato's *Republic* the philosopher-kings, the Guardians, rule; the military class, the Auxiliaries, maintains order and provides defence; the Producers, the common people, are responsible for the material basis of society. H. G. Wells's *A Modern Utopia* echoes this Platonic conception with its tripartite division into the Poietic (the creative and spiritual ruling class, the Samurai), the Kinetic (the executive-administrative class), and the Base (not so much the workers, as work is mostly mechanized, but more a residual uncreative mass which is steadily being reduced). Aldous Huxley's anti-utopia, *Brave New World* (1932), parodies this utopian tradition with its laboratory-produced Alpha, Beta, Gamma and Epsilon castes.

The functional division of labour by occupation is frequently accompanied by a topographical division of the ideal city into specialized regions. This was a marked feature of virtually all Renaissance utopias, no doubt here echoing the practice of the mediaeval as much as the ancient city. In Andreae's *Christianopolis* (1619) the spiritual functions are concentrated at the centre of the city, the site of the temple; the more material the task, the more distant its physical site, in successive zones radiating out from the centre. Campanella's *City of the Sun* (1623) is divided into seven concentric circles; a temple at the centre marks the site of spiritual and political power. Each circle, segregated by walls from the others, contains the homes and workshops of artisans specialized in particular branches of the arts and manufactures. Taken together the seven circles can be seen as a repository of all the skills and materials needed for the life of the city.

Campanella's City of the Sun illustrates a further feature of the ideal city. The city is a total, self-sufficient entity, at least so far as its spiritual and creative purposes go. Peasants might provision it but they play no real part in its basic function of ordering and promoting the good life, the life of the mind and spirit. The walls dividing up the seven circles of the City of the Sun are covered, in words and pictures, with the totality of human knowledge. The city is the physical embodiment of all the arts and sciences known to man. It is a compendium of all knowledge, all that is needed for the cultivation of the good life.

Philosophy and science realized in stone – Plato himself might have admired this attempt to eternalize the ideal. The political and social institutions of men decay more rapidly than the cities they inhabit (Rome, with the physical remnants of many civilizations, must have been a particularly telling example to Renaissance thinkers). Might it not be possible to stave off corruption by the careful design of the physical environment? Architecture has always been the most utopian of all the arts. In modern times it has been the main carrier of the ideal-city tradition. From the architectural utopias of Alberti and Leonardo in the Renaissance, to Le Corbusier's designs for the 'city of tomorrow', architects and urban planners have sought to realize the good life in the bricks of buildings and the grids of squares and streets.[18]

The Renaissance urbanists, steeped in Platonism, aimed to establish in their centralized, circular cities the hierarchical and aristocratic order of the *Republic*. L'Enfant's plan for Washington DC was informed by the classicism and rationalism of the eighteenth-century Enlightenment. Reacting against industrialism, the garden city movement of Patrick Geddes and Ebenezer Howard at the end of the nineteenth century sought to combine the best of town and country. Twentieth-century modernists such as Le

Corbusier and Mies van der Rohe, on the contrary, looked to advanced industrial technology for the construction of dense and highly concentrated urban spaces in which all activities were integrated in one tightly knit pattern. This reversion to Platonism – Le Corbusier wished to create 'a single society, united in belief and action' – produced in its turn a democratic and populist reaction. The International Situationists of the 1950s and 1960s rejected rigid urban planning and called for the creation of fluid urban 'situations' in which people could create their own spontaneous forms of life ('do their own thing').

The libertarian urban utopia of the Situationists, prominent in the 1968 May Events in Paris, was a measure of how far the ideal city had travelled since its conception in the ancient Hellenic world. It reflected perhaps the changing role of the city in society. So long as the city was basically coterminous with society, as it was in the city-states of the ancient world, the ideal city retained the ordered, regulated character that was its principal hallmark. The city was everything; it performed all political, social and economic functions; its life therefore must be carefully organized and watched over. Renaissance thinkers, themselves wholehearted urbanists, reasserted the primacy of the city against the anarchic countryside. Their utopias pitted reason against the formless chaos of nature. The utopian city of the Renaissance, with its radial plan and centralized pattern, was like the Hellenic ideal city a microcosm not just of human society but of the whole cosmic order.

The rise of the nation-state, and later of industrialism, reduced the city to a part of a larger, more complex social organism. Industrial society is certainly urban society; but it is also national and increasingly international society. The industrial city becomes a specialized segment within a highly differentiated division of labour on a national and international plane. One city may largely carry on production; another may be specialized for services; a third may concentrate governmental functions (e.g. Detroit, New York, Washington DC in the United States). The specialization within the nation-state may be replicated on a global scale – for instance, the industrial cities of south-east Asia are serviced and to a large extent regulated by the metropolitan cities of Europe and North America. In the modern age cities multiply and their populations increase; but no longer can they aspire to be the concentrated expression of the whole human or cosmic order.

In this new pattern the ideal city, too, has room to change its form. The older visions persist, as we can see in Le Corbusier; but they are increasingly accompanied by alternative conceptions which reflect the changed role of the city. The sovereignty of the city is broken by the introduction of non-urban elements. The garden city movement brought the country into the city; William Morris's *News from Nowhere* (1890) balances Arcadia against small market towns conceived on a mediaeval pattern. In Frank Lloyd Wright's utopian Broadacre City (1934) houses are widely dispersed and the private car is the principal link between individualized households. The city has become suburbs, *urbs in rure*.

What is important in urban life also changes in the newer visions. The ideal cities of the recent era are concerned as much with consumption as with production, with leisure as much as work, with family life as much as politics. They largely accept the basic distinction between private and public life. The city is the site of leisure, spontaneity, fun. It offers opportunities for thrills and exotic experiences. The ultimate expression of this is the ideal city as Disneyland, given formal status by Walt Disney in his last years in his design for the utopian city of Epcot.

From Plato to Walt Disney is indeed a leap; and it illustrates the variety of the ideal city tradition. Still, both the Republic and Epcot share the essential feature of being systematically designed environments. It was this supreme idealization of reason that ensured that the *Republic* remained the most influential carrier of the ideal city tradition, long after the city-state had ceased to occupy the central place in the social order. It was the more influential for supposedly representing the actual life of some famous cities of the ancient world. The *Republic* itself is notoriously vague as to the precise physical and social arrangements of the ideal city. But at other times Plato was at pains to emphasize the concreteness and even practicability of his vision. In the *Timaeus* and the *Critias* he outlines the ideal city-empire of Atlantis before its fall, giving such details as its beautiful landscape and its abundant natural resources. He also portrays, as a great and good society, the original Athenian community that was Atlantis's conqueror and successor. Plato suggests that both these ancient, semi-mythical cities were actual historical prefigurations of the ideal city of the *Republic*. Later, in the *Laws*, he draws repeatedly on the historic institutions of Crete and Sparta, again giving concrete historical referents for his ideal society. Nor has it escaped commentators that the ideal order of the Republic itself was indebted to the practices of the Pythagorean communities of southern Italy in the sixth and fifth centuries BC. These philosophically governed model communities, 'the most famous utopian experiment of the ancient world',[19] were the clearest indication of the practicability of societies ruled by rational philosophy. It was a view, however, that had to be set against Plato's own disastrous intervention in the politics of Syracuse: a disillusioning experience that seems to have made him question whether the whole idea of the ideal city was an earthly possibility.

The making of utopia

There are other kinds of ideal societies: the lost continent of Atlantis, the hidden valley of Shangri-La, the distant country of El Dorado, the Land-Without-Evil of the Guarani Indians, the life of 'the noble savage', fabulous civilizations at the centre of the earth and on the moon. Times past and times future, other-worldly regions and distant planets – all have been the setting in myth, romance and science fiction for innumerable ideal societies.

Ideal-society types also clearly overlap one another. Paradise is fused with the Golden Age; Cockaygne is a reproach to Arcadia while it borrows heavily from the Golden Age and Paradise; the millennium is Paradise restored; the ideal city draws upon the myths of ancient Golden Age civilizations. The religious connotations of many of these terms also point to their interconnection within overarching religious cosmologies.

Do all these types add up to utopia? Is utopia no more than an amalgam of older ideal society conceptions? Or is it a distinct variety, with its own features and its own tradition? If so, how might we distinguish it from other varieties?

The argument of the next chapter is that utopia is indeed distinct and different from other types of ideal society. Here, though, we can note what may be thought to be the 'elemental' contribution of the principal varieties of the ideal society to the utopian idea. By this is meant not so much that utopia is constructed directly out of these elements as that they have infused into it certain sentiments, images and themes. In the making of utopia they may be thought of as residues, in Pareto's sense, or as archetypes or unconscious strivings in the psychology of Jung and Freud. None of this, however, should be taken as implying any innate or fixed human propensity to utopia.

At the most elementary level, as a primary driving force, Cockaygne contributes the element of desire. It portrays a world of unrestrained enjoyment and pleasure, the libido at large and in charge. On its own, as a realized project, Cockaygne would rapidly lead to excess and satiety, probably also to killing and riotous disorder, as in some of its Saturnalian forms. But the absence of scarcity and the joyful abundance of all that is desired – especially food and sex – drive out these darker shades. If utopia is longed for, if it promises the escape from toil and suffering, then Cockaygne is the ingredient that supplies the essential instinctual charge.

Paradise and the Golden Age contribute the element of harmony. Human beings live in a state of quiet contentment. Everyone is at peace with himself and with other men. The order of creation is one. Human beings live in and according to nature. This is life before the fall into alienation, of man from man, man from nature and man from God. Simplicity is the keynote of this order. It is by the restriction of needs that so few demands are made on nature and society. If Cockaygne inflates desire and so prompts discord, Paradise and the Golden Age conceive man as naturally a creature of few and simple needs and desires, readily satisfied by the bounty of nature. The Paradisiac image of a peaceful garden, with its fruits, trees, water, birds and other animals, is the perfect representation of this condition of primal innocence and natural harmony. In so far as utopia strives for stability, for an order of unchanging perfection, then Paradise and the Golden Age are the images that underpin this vision.

The millennium contributes the element of hope. Salvation is assured, if not now then certainly at some time in the future. Strife and suffering may be the current condition of mankind, but this not to be forever. An end to them will come. The eschatalogical hope of the millennium sustains the believer in the midst of catastrophe and cataclysm. These may even be welcomed as the signs or symptoms of the coming new order. Millenarianism can induce either passive waiting or active preparation for the new order but in neither case can it ever lead to cynicism or despair. Sooner or later, peacefully or violently, the new dispensation must make its appearance and justice and freedom reign. If utopia is a serious speculation about the possibility of human betterment, it is the millennium that supplies the ingredient of hope without which such speculation becomes an idle fancy or an intellectual game.

The ideal city contributes the element of design. Its premise is that the good society must be constructed, thought through in a systematic way. It hallmark is reason, its emblem the plan. In the ideal city tradition, man as philosopher – architect – artisan is joint creator with Jove. Like God, and given reason by Him, man must legislate according to conscious purpose. As little as possible must be left to chance. The ideal city seeks to contain and control every possibility within its walls. It is a compendium of all the arts, practical and political as well as poetic and philosophic. If, as many have held, the basic feature of utopia is the blueprint or plan, it is the ideal city that has bequeathed that legacy.

Desire and design, harmony and hope: these certainly go into the making of utopia, as probably with any other social and political philosophy. Their particular carriers are therefore undoubtedly important in its construction. But utopia does not simply recombine these elements. It has its own inventiveness. Once established, it provides a map of quite different possibilities for speculating on the human condition.

The Boundaries of Utopia

Imaginary worlds

When we encounter utopia the first thing we encounter in most cases is a story. Utopia distinguishes itself from other forms of the ideal society, and from other forms of social and political theory, by being in the first place a piece of fiction. It is, using the term in its broadest sense, a species of 'science fiction'.

Plato in the *Timaeus* and the *Critias* wrote what is probably the earliest work of science fiction in his account of the civilization of Atlantis and its rivalry with ancient Athens. Both societies are invented ideal societies, and both are clothed with the kind of detail we expect from story-tellers. The device by which the account is introduced is equally a typical piece of literary artifice. Critias recounts a tale told to him by his grandfather, who in turn heard it from his own father's relative and friend Solon, who himself heard it during his travels in Egypt where, as Solon is gently reminded, historical records go back far further than in his own country. Thus the 'great point in its favour', as Socrates remarks of the tale, is that, 'it is not a fiction but true history.'[1]

The story goes that there once existed a mighty civilization in the Atlantic, an island empire which gave the ocean its name. Atlantis is described as a wondrous isle, with high mountains and fertile plains, and abounding in natural resources. Among these is the valuable metal 'orichalc' – 'which survives today only in name' – which adorns the many beautiful buildings of Atlantis. Atlantis is a highly developed technological civilization. Plato goes into painstaking detail on the planning and construction of its capital city. At the centre is the inner citadel containing the royal palace and, separated by a golden wall, the vast but 'somewhat outlandish' temple of Poseidon. Around it is the rest of the city, ranged in concentric circles. Elaborate bridges and aqueducts link the capital city to the other islands in the Atlantic empire. There is also an intricate system of canals, for communication and irrigation, connecting the whole network. In the surrounding countryside, 'numerous elephants' among the island's fauna add an exotic touch.

Atlantis was originally peaceful and just.

> They bore the burden of their wealth and possessions lightly, and did not let their high standard of living intoxicate them or make them lose their self-control, but saw soberly and clearly that all these things flourish only on a soil of common goodwill and individual character, and if pursued too eagerly and overvalued destroy themselves and morality with them.[2]

Atlantis is to this extent therefore itself an ideal society. But gradually it succumbed to the very evil it feared. It became puffed up with wealth and power and sought to dominate its Mediterranean neighbours to the east. This brought it into conflict with ancient Athens. Athens, even more than Atlantis, represents the original ideal city. It was, Solon's Egyptian informant tells him, the city 'conspicuously the best governed in every way, its achievements and constitution being the finest of any in the world of which we have heard tell'.[3]

While Atlantis is strong on technology, Athens is dedicated to learning and morality. It maintains a strict separation of functions between the different orders, priests, artisans, and soldiers. The military order – the Guardians – has a specially elevated role as the custodians of the temple and rulers of the city. But they are a communal order with no individual possessions and little collective wealth. They are more like scholar-monks than soldiers. They lead an austere and rather ascetic life, concerned not so much with nurturing warlike qualities as with the cultivation and pursuit of 'the divine principles of cosmology' which regulate and guide all the actions of the city. In ancient Athens, as in the *Republic*, philosophy rules.

Athens leads an alliance of Greek cities against Atlantis. She is quickly deserted by them but fights on alone and emerges victorious. Generously she restores freedom in the Mediterranean. Solon's Egyptian informant recounts the subsequent fate of the two great antagonists.

At a later time there were earthquakes and floods of extraordinary
violence, and in a single dreadful day and night all your [i.e. the
Athenian] fighting men were swallowed up by the earth, and the
island of Atlantis was similarly swallowed up by the sea and vanished;
this is why the sea in that area is to this day impassable to navigation,
which is hindered by mud just below the surface, the remains of the
sunken island.[4]

How far the *Timaeus* and the *Critias* – and indeed the *Republic* –
are 'true' utopias will concern us later. Here the important thing is
the presentation of undeniably ideal societies within the framework
of a narrative. Its importance is of course heightened by the
enormous influence of the myth of Atlantis in the later utopian
tradition – Bacon after all called his utopia New Atlantis.[5] But the
form is as significant as the content. Plato tells a story of magnificent
cities, mythical metals, extraordinary buildings, outlandish crea-
tures, noble heroism, war, earthquakes, floods, an impassable
ocean and a sunken continent. In the midst of this he portrays –
admittedly in very sketchy form – two societies which have achieved
something like an ideal form. Whether or not Plato actually
believed in the existence of Atlantis – plausibly identified these days
with Minoan Crete – his ancient Athens is clearly a deliberate
fiction. In any case both societies are embellished and elaborated
for didactic purposes. They are represented as concrete, historically
specific societies. In the 'true history' of Atlantis and Athens, Plato
seeks to show the ideal society in action.

At the opening of the *Timaeus* Socrates recapitulates the features
of an ideal society which he had discussed with his guests the day
before. This ideal society is close to that of the *Republic*. Socrates
expresses a certain dissatisfaction with this way – his way – of
presenting the ideal society.

My feelings are rather like those of a man who has seen some
splendid animals, either in a picture or really alive but motionless,
and wants to see them moving and engaging in some of the activities
for which they appear to be formed. That's exactly what I feel about
the society we have described. I would be glad to hear some account
of it engaging in transactions with other states, waging war success-
fully and showing in the process all the qualities one would expect
from its system of education and training, both in action and in
negotiation with its rivals.[6]

It is important that Socrates as a speculative philosopher feels that he cannot himself provide the account that he desires. He can supply the intellectual scaffolding but not the realized structures of the ideal city. Nor, he says, is he interested in the fanciful fabrications of the poets. It is to people like Timaeus and Critias that he turns: men of substance and worldly experience, men who have travelled and seen the ways of the great cities of the world, men who have been statesmen and administrators. These men possess practical knowledge as well as philosophic wisdom. It is men such as they who out of their concrete experience can animate the ideal society with the colourful details of its buildings and art, the everyday life of its people, how it conducts family life and the relations between men and women, its politics and its encounters with other states. Only by such an account, Socrates seems to suggest, and not through the abstract systems of philosophers, will the ideal society enter the minds and emotions of men.

Nearly two thousand years later, it was to a practical man, Ralph Hythloday, a traveller with much experience of distant lands, that More also turned for the account of the ideal society of the island of Utopia. More was clearly influenced by the 'traveller's tale' literature flooding Europe in the wake of the Portuguese and Spanish voyages of discovery. His own offering is in direct and conscious imitation of that literature. But he was also profoundly aware of Plato's example. Although a fervent admirer of the *Republic* More is proud, as a poem 'in the Utopian tongue' claims, to have shaped 'a philosophical city . . . without philosophy' – that is, without the aid of an abstract philosophical system. The Utopian poet laureate Anemolius, speaking in the name of Utopia, praises it for having 'excelled and passed' Plato's city.

> For what Plato's pen hath platted [sketched] briefly
> In naked words, as in a glass,
> The same have I performed fully,
> With laws, with men, and treasure fitly.

Anemolius's poem boldly claims that to have depicted a world so vividly is to lift it out of the realm of 'nowhere' and turn it into a real, a living place.

> Wherefore not Utopie, but rather rightly
> My name is Eutopie: a place of felicity.[7]

The presentation of life in Utopia in all its density and concrete particularity becomes a way of more forcibly treating discursive and theoretical issues whose matter is otherwise inescapably shot through with prejudice and uncertainty. When it is objected to Hythloday that communism of property must be a disincentive to work and so lead to material poverty, his first response is an appeal not to theory but to the day to day life of the Utopians as experienced and observed by him: 'You should have been with me in Utopia and personally seen their manners and customs as I did . . .'[8] Hythloday proposes to convince his doubting friends not by arguing speculatively about communism but by showing its effects in as wide a range of Utopian institutions and practices as possible. His friends in return, graciously conceding the possible merit of this way of advancing the discussion, urge him not to stint but but to give as complete and elaborated an account of Utopia as he can. 'Study not to be short, but declare largely in order their rivers, their cities, their people, their manners, their ordinances, their laws . . .'[9] Utopia is to be promoted not by the elaboration of arid theory but by the telling of a story. It will be a tale of a strange and wondrous land, which will allow the narrator all the artful resources of vivid scenes and extraordinary doings, feigned incomprehension and telling comparison.

More here follows the Plato of the *Critias* rather than of the *Republic*. He has wished to portray a world that ordinary people, rather than simply philosophers, can imagine themselves living in. His purpose, like Plato's, remains didactic. His *Utopia*, he wrote to his friend Peter Giles, was 'a fiction whereby the truth, as if smeared with honey, might a little more pleasantly slide into men's minds.'[10] Sir Philip Sidney, in *A Defence of Poetry* (1595), chose More's *Utopia* as an example of the superiority of fiction (poetry) over history in teaching goodness. The point is clear: Utopia is primarily a vehicle of social and political speculation rather than an exercise of the literary imagination in and for itself. It is meant to engage our sympathies and our desires in the direction favoured by the writer.

This is, of course, true of most works of literature. The difference perhaps has more to do with emphasis and a more deliberate and direct political intent in the case of utopian literature. Certainly More's own example has meant that the literary form of utopia has been far broader than a simple didactic tale. The layers and levels of meaning in *Utopia*, its teasing allusiveness, its wit and sparkle, from the very first demonstrated that utopia as a literary form was capable of carrying many complex meanings. Plato's *Critias* is a mere fragment (and the *Laws* followed a different direction); it took More's *Utopia* to show the possibilities of narrative fiction as a means of conveying the ideal society in all its complexity and density.

All utopias are by definition, fictions; unlike say historical writing, they deal with possible, not actual, worlds. To this extent they are like all forms of imaginative literature.[11] They go further than conventional fiction in their extension of the bounds of the possible to include what to many may seem impossible or at least very improbable. Their fiction, that is, belongs more to the genre of science fiction than that of the conventional realist or naturalistic novel.[12] But for all that they remain in the world of fiction and share its main features. They are not, for instance, to be judged by a straightforward appeal to history or contemporary life for their 'truth' or validity – but no more than other kinds of novels can they ignore history or social reality.

The utopia as devised by More is best seen as a kind of novel. Indeed, it undoubtedly contributed to the development of the novel in its more conventional form as it emerged in the eighteenth century. Once fully formed the novel in its turn fed utopia by extending its range and possibilities. Wells once wrote that it behoved the utopian (or science fiction) writer to try 'to domesticate the impossible hypothesis' if he were to have any hope of carrying the reader with him. The realist novel of the eighteenth and nineteenth centuries offered a vast repertoire of techniques for at least 'domesticating the improbable', and so supplied many of the necessary technical devices to utopian writers. David Lodge has suggested that the influence goes even deeper.

> For the orthodox realistic novelist the creation of a plausible 'world' densely specified and historically consistent, is usually the frame within which he explores imaginary characters and actions that are the main focus of interest. It only needs a small adjustment to make the frame imaginary and the main focus of interest, and the characters and actions of importance mainly as filling out and authenticating the frame. This is what happens in most modern utopian and science fiction. The conventions of the realistic novel can thus invest the imaginary frame with an astonishing pseudo-historical verisimilitude, so that Orwell's London of 1984, for instance, seems

just as 'real' as Dickens' London or Zola's Paris. We experience it
from within. The future is enacted before us in the continuous
present of the narrative past tense.[13]

More's *Utopia* was a distinctive literary invention that effectively
marked out the field of utopia for the next five hundred years. There
are divisions to be made within that history, as we shall see; but
what is more striking is the continuity of form over so long a period.
More's traveller journeyed to Utopia across the surface of the
earth; others have travelled through time, made voyages to distant
planets, dreamt or slept their way into utopia. Whatever the
manner of the arrival, how they describe their utopias has usually
followed the Morean pattern closely. For all the obvious differences
of content, More would have had little difficulty in recognizing the
basic utopian form in Bellamy's *Looking Backward* (1888), Morris's *News from Nowhere* (1890), or Wells's *Men Like Gods* (1923);
while what would have struck him about most of the routine science
fiction utopias of the twentieth century – such as James Hilton's
Lost Horizon (1933) – was not their novelty but their poverty of
imagination.

The constancy of the utopian form should not be thought to entail
a simple uniformity. The basic narrative pattern – a visitor from
another place or time encounters a superior civilization – allows for
considerable virtuosity of treatment. There is room for comic
misunderstanding, thwarted intrigue, romance. Satire, the holding
up of an unflattering mirror to one's own society, has ever since
More been the stock in trade of utopia and given it some of its
sharpest barbs (e.g. in *Utopia* gold and silver are used exclusively
for chamberpots and prisoners' chains).[14] There is scope too for a
darker theme of frustration and bitterness (particularly marked in
Morris and Wells) as the visitor gains in consciousness of the new
ways, and reflects on his own stunted development and that of his
fellows as products of the old society. And a device used to
especially telling effect in Bellamy and Wells is the nightmare return
– in dream or reality – to the visitor's own society, now bathed in a
ghastly and hellish light (see the end of *Looking Backward* and *A
Modern Utopia*).

The satirical strand in utopia eventually led to the splitting off of a
separate sub-genre, the dystopia or anti-utopia.[15] The negative,
critical pole of satire could be fully developed on its own, without a

corresponding positive pole, to show a society marked by the extremes of folly and unreason. Swift's *Gulliver's Travels* (1726) exhilaratingly led the way, to be followed in a similar vein by Samuel Butler's *Erewhon* (1872). Later, as the modern scientific and industrial utopia came to seem to many only too realizable and imminent, anti-utopia concerned itself less with mockery and ridicule and sought instead to terrify and appal. In Wells's early anti-utopian novels (such as *The Time Machine*, 1895, and *The Island of Dr Moreau*, 1896), in Zamyatin's *We* (1920), Huxley's *Brave New World* (1932), and Orwell's *Nineteen Eighty-Four* (1949), the anti-utopian form drew on all the techniques of the modern novel to present a chilling vision of an alienated and enslaved world. The anti-utopia, like its parent the utopia, showed the vitality and versatility of the form not simply as a vehicle for social and political ideas but as a literary expression of genuine power.

Utopia, then, is first and foremost a work of imaginative fiction in which, unlike other such works, the central subject is the good society. This distinguishes it at the same time from other treatments of the good society, whether in myths of a Golden Age, beliefs in a coming millennium, or philosophical speculation on the ideal city. Fictive elements no doubt have their part to play in these modes but in none of them is narrative fiction, as in the utopia, the defining form.

Utopia and utopian theory

For some commentators utopia is exclusively defined by its form as imaginative fiction.[16] Most, however, have evidently felt that while this may be its primary feature, other kinds of thinking also belong to the utopian canon. They may be prepared to accept that utopia differs from some of the older expressions of the ideal society, such as millenarianism. But few writers have found it possible to discuss utopia at any length without discussing such thinkers as Rousseau, Owen, Saint-Simon and Marx. Yet none of these thinkers wrote what the Manuels call a 'speaking picture utopia' – a utopia proper, a story of the ideal society.[17] They can be ranged easily enough alongside the Plato of the *Republic* but less comfortably alongside the Plato of the *Critias*. At the side of More and his *Utopia* they look

distinctly awkward. Why then has it become customary to include
them in most surveys of utopias? And should we?
  J. C. Davis has said that

> all political philosophy deals in fictions- 'sovereignty', 'the dialectic',
> 'general will', 'separation of powers', 'public opinion', 'common
> good'. Fiction then may be seen as an attribute of utopian writing
> only in the same sense that it is an attribute of all political
> theorising.[18]

To this it can reasonably be objected that anyone can tell the
difference between the fiction, say, of Morris's *News from Nowhere*
and that of Locke's *Two Treatises of Government*. But the point is
nevertheless a serious one. The imaginative fiction of utopia may be
its most distinctive – and valuable – feature, but it is possible that
other kinds of fiction, not always seen as such, may profitably be
considered as utopian. This may also have the advantage that it
allows us to specify other features of utopia. Utopia is a story of
what it is to encounter and experience the good society. But what is
the nature of that good society? How does the utopian good society
differ from other conceptions and traditions of the good society?
Here it may be helpful to add to utopia, as an additional or
supplementary category, the genre of 'utopian theory' or 'utopian
thought'.[19]
  All expressions of social and political theory may be fictions, but
they are not all fictions of the same kind. They can differ not simply
in their form – the dialogue, the treatise, the advice to princes – but
also in their fundamental assumptions about human nature and its
possibilities. This is probably the best way of distinguishing utopian
theory from other kinds of social theory. Most social theory
assumes that order and happiness are problematic in human society
because of inherent defects of human nature or the human
condition. Men, it is held, are naturally aggressive or acquisitive.
They always think of themselves first and of others only much later,
if at all. Their natural impulse is to make of others the servants of
their will. But since their purposes can only be realized jointly, in
society, they give up their individual liberty and live together as best
they can, in more or less unsatisfactory and imperfect relationships.
The 'vexatious fact of society', a situation in which frustrations and
conflict are inherent and endemic, defines the human condition.
Order and cooperation may be harshly imposed, by some such

agency as Hobbes's Leviathan; or they may be more agreeably arrived at by the kind of liberal arrangements proposed by Locke or Mill. But the keynote of both these – and other – kinds of society is precariousness and provisionality. Human beings will constantly seek, even against their own best interest, to evade laws and institutional norms. Human social order is a constant battle against selfishness and the plunge into anarchy. At best it can lay down some ground rules for softening the terms and conditions of that battle.

Utopian social theory rejects these assumptions about the human condition. Utopians do not necessarily believe in the natural goodness of man – else why should utopian arrangements be necessary at all – but they do believe in his more or less indefinite malleability. What links More's *Utopia* to, say, Robert Owen's *A New View of Society* (1813), and separates both from say Hobbes's *Leviathan* and Locke's *Two Treatises*, is the conviction that humanity is perfectible.[20] This may be qualified – but not too much – by something like the belief in original sin; and the notion of perfectibility will of course be interpreted in different ways by different people at different times. But what unites utopians, and gives to utopian theory its distinctive emphasis, is the assumption that there is nothing in man, nature or society that cannot be so ordered as to bring about a more or less permanent state of material plenty, social harmony and individual fulfilment. There are no fundamental barriers or obstacles to man's earthly perfection. Scarcity can be overcome; conflict can be eliminated; moral dilemmas and psychological frustrations can be resolved. Men can, in short, become gods (if not God). What need then for 'politics', understood as the power struggles of a materially straitened and socially divided world? The frequently noted contempt for politics in utopian theory is the logical complement of its belief in perfectibility.

Taking this belief as a yardstick, we might instance the following works as examples of utopian theory. None of these works is a formal utopia, but they can all reasonably be distinguished from conventional social theory as being the products of the utopian temperament or the utopian propensity. There is Rousseau's attempt, in *The Social Contract* (1762), to show how the virtues of the primitive golden age of mankind can be fully carried over into a moral commonwealth where the individual will harmonizes perfectly with the general will. There is the utopian enterprise of the

Enlightenment *philosophes* as a whole, in their endeavour to build a heavenly city on earth out of the bricks of reason and science. Here we need to include not just formal utopias such as Diderot's *Supplement to Bougainville's Voyage* (1796), but also William Godwin's rationalist treatise, *Political Justice* (1793), as well as the extravagant vision of moral and sexual liberation in the Marquis de Sade's *Philosophy of the Bedroom* (1795). There is also the crucial linking of utopia to time and history in the eighteenth-century idea of progress, as in Turgot's *Discourses on the Advancement of the Human Race and Mind* (1750) and Condorcet's *Sketch for a Historical Picture of the Progress of the Human Mind* (1793).

This is continued in the great philosophies of history in the nineteenth century, in the works of Saint-Simon, Comte, Hegel and Marx, where human history is seen to culminate in 'the return of man to himself' and the full realization of mental and moral powers in a totally reconstituted and emancipated world. Matching these are the visions of the utopian socialists, as in Robert Owen's *A New View of Society* and Charles Fourier's *Le Nouveau Monde Industriel et Sociétaire* (1829). Later, picking up partly from de Sade and rebutting Freud's pessimism, there are the 'eupsychias' or psycho-logical utopias of Erich Fromm (*The Fear of Freedom*, *The Sane Society*), Norman O'Brown (*Life Against Death*), and Herbert Marcuse (*Eros and Civilization*, *An Essay on Liberation*). A parallel movement met the challenge of Darwin in the biological utopia, starting with Winwood Reade's *The Martyrdom of Man* (1872), and continuing with J. D. Bernal's *The World, the Flesh and the Devil* (1929), and Teilhard de Chardin's *The Phenomenon of Man* (1959).[21]

The diversity of these examples of utopian theory is itself a problem. Moreover it would be wrong to pretend that the line dividing utopian theory from other kinds of social theory is either very clear or consistent. Individual theorists easily cross from one side to the other. Locke's *Some Thoughts Concerning Education* (1693), for instance, with its belief in the unbounded possibilities of education, might well appear to some utopian;[22] while on the other hand there is a distinct sense in Rousseau that the real utopia of mankind, the age of the noble savage, is lost forever, and that even the best of modern societies must by comparison be second rate. Marx, too, might be instanced as a thinker in whom utopia warred constantly with a more sceptical and even pessimistic bent. The inspired utopianism of the *Economic and Philosophical Manuscripts*, for instance, and of parts of *The German Ideology*, is countered by the scornful attacks on the utopianism of anarchists such as Proudhon and Bakunin, and by the 'realistic' dismissal of utopian experiments in socialism of the Owenite and Fourierist kind.

In the end it comes down to a question of usefulness. We will classify our material in different ways according to particular purposes. It may be helpful to separate out a branch of social theory as utopian social theory, and to consider it alongside the formal literary utopia. Or it may on other occasions be important to stress that all social theory is utopian or has a utopian dimension, and that it is improper to distinguish a particular category of utopian social theory. All social theory, it can readily be shown, deals in imaginary worlds where impossibly pure or ideal principles reign: states where sovereignty is actually operative, constitutions where powers are truly divided, democracies where the people really rule. The fiction of social theory does not in this respect differ much from the fiction of utopia.

It is certainly easy to see why, faced with this, certain commentators such as Bertrand de Jouvenel are firm that 'the designation of "Utopia" should be denied to any exposition of a "New Model" of Society which is bereft of pictures concerning daily life.'[23] Only the utopia proper, the fiction of a journey to a new world, with the detailed description of the daily life of its inhabitants, is to be admitted to the utopian canon. This is not so much a matter of wishing to make the literary imagination the principal feature of utopian writing. More importantly, it is to suggest that utopia and formal social theory – including utopian social theory – are also separated by a fundamental difference in their modes of social analysis.

In the abstract schemes of conventional social and political theory, we are *told* that the good society will follow from the application of the relevant general principles; in utopia we are *shown* the good society in operation, supposedly as a result of certain general principles of social organization. We may or may not be convinced that the life so glowingly depicted will in fact follow from the application of the principles. Notoriously in the socialist utopia, for instance, the same general principles of socialism lead to the quite different societies of Edward Bellamy's *Looking Backward* and William Morris's *News from Nowhere*. But at least we know, in the case of any individual utopian writer, what the results, spelled out in terms of everyday life, are supposed to look like. The utopian writer provides, usually in vivid and abundant detail, the evidence by which we can judge the desirability and practicability of any scheme of social reconstruction. In the case of abstract social theory there remains a fundamental ambiguity as to the concrete social order that is to emerge from the application of general principles. We know what Bellamy or Morris – or Cabet – thought socialism would be like; what did Marx think socialism would be like? Marx's contemptuous dismissal of utopias – 'I write no recipes for the cookshops of the future' – had to be paid for heavily by the later socialist movement.

So there is, compared with abstract social theory, a basic honesty and transparency in utopia's way of doing sociology and social philosophy.[24] That in itself may be enough to persuade some commentators to leave utopian theory alone and stick to the formal literary utopia. But there is no need, here or anywhere else in the human sciences, to be dogmatic or exclusive about concepts. Their deployment is mainly a matter of our use and convenience. It may make good sense, for instance, to treat Marx's utopianism along with that of More or Plato. Certainly the common theme of communism is sufficient to suggest influences and affinities, while at the same time promising to show up interesting differences. The fact that neither Marx nor Plato ever wrote a proper 'speaking picture' utopia cannot be adequate grounds for banning them forever from the realm of utopia. Given their undoubted standing there such a procedure would in any case be self-defeating.

Utopia in time and space

It may seem quaint to question at all the place of Plato in the utopian tradition. Is it not the merest commonplace that in the *Republic* Plato wrote the archetypal utopia? That all utopias subsequently have been so indebted to it as to seem merely slavish imitations?[25]

Plato is undoubtedly important, but not necessarily as the inventor or creator of the utopian form. Similarly Christianity is important in utopia even though in most essential respects utopia is a distinctively secular type of social thought. Finally, although ideas such as the Golden Age, Paradise, the Land of Cockaygne and the

Millennium are to be found in many cultures, only in the West do we find utopia and a utopian tradition.

Utopia, in short, has temporal and spatial as well as conceptual boundaries. Or perhaps it would be better to say that the concept is defined by its appearance at a certain point in history, within a certain intellectual and cultural tradition. Unlike the case with the natural sciences, concepts in the human sciences have no timeless essence. They are the products of particular histories and particular interpretations of those histories. Their meaning can change with time and with the diversity of uses to which they may be put. This does not mean that usage can or should be arbitrary. There are generally certain formal and thematic continuities, as we shall see with utopia in the next chapter. But it does mean that we should neither expect nor seek some universal or essentialist definition valid for all times and places. In the case of utopia, in particular, we need to acknowledge the importance of distinctions of time and place in establishing its character.

When Thomas More coined the word utopia in 1516 he invented more than a new word, he invented a new form. His *Utopia* is different from anything that had appeared before in the classical or Christian world. It is also different from anything we find in the non-Western world.

To take the second point first, since it is so large a topic that we must be brutally brief. There is no tradition of utopia and utopian thought outside the Western world. Other varieties of the ideal society or the perfect condition of humanity are to be found in abundance in non-Western societies, usually embedded in religious cosmologies.[26] But nowhere in these societies do we find the practice of writing utopias, of criticizing them, of developing and transforming their themes and exploring new possibilities within them. Even if individual works can be found with some of the hallmarks of the Western utopia – and that too can be disputed – there is no utopian tradition of thought.

Only for China has it seriously ever been claimed that there is something approaching an indigenous utopian tradition, independent of Western influences.[27] But on inspection it turns out that what we are presented with are predominantly primitivist conceptions whose central feature is a lost Golden Age. The chief candidates are the ancient Taoist concepts of *Ta Thung* and *Thai Phing*.[28]

Ta Thung refers to the state or period of 'Great Togetherness' or 'Great Unity'. 'When the Great Tao prevailed, the whole world was one Community.' It harked back to a Golden Age of primitive agrarian communism, an age of equality, justice and social harmony. Essentially it was a vision of a tribal paradise before the coming of state, bureaucracy and social classes. As the ideology of poor peasant farmers it was a powerful rallying call in the many peasant rebellions of dynastic China. For Sun Yat-Sen and Mao Tse-Tung, intent on finding indigenous roots for their modern revolutionary movements, *Ta Thung* could be one of the building blocks of Chinese socialism or Chinese communism.

Thai Phing is the age or condition of Great Peace and Equality. This too mainly looked back to a Golden Age, but in successive commentaries it came to include elements of a future state which would restore something of the happiness of the original *Thai Phing*. Like the Roman Emperors who proclaimed that their reigns would or had reestablished the Golden Age, new dynastic rulers in China frequently announced that their accession had inaugurated the restoration of the Great Peace. *Thai Phing*, like *Ta Thung*, was regularly invoked by peasant rebels, notably in the great *Thai Phing* rebellion of the mid-nineteenth century.

Confucian scholars reworked these two concepts into an incipient theory of evolution and progress. Tung Chung-Shu's concept of the *San Shih* or Three Ages was developed by Ho Hsiu into an evolutionary series in which a new *Thai Phing* was announced as imminent. This is the main basis of the claim that social thought in China was not always and only primitivist but contained notions of time, history and progress.[29]

Whatever the truth of this it is a far cry from genuine utopianism. A theory of progress, even one much more developed than the rudimentary Confucian one, is not the same as utopia. In the Chinese version, too, it is almost always coupled with messianic and millenarian expectations associated with the Buddhist *Maitreya* or *Mi-Lo-Fu*. In any case, reflection on *Ta Thung* and *Thai Phing* did not give rise to a literary tradition of composing utopias based on their vision of the good life. They remained backward-looking ideological slogans, useful for protest, like 'the Norman Yoke'. While such looking back certainly has an important place in utopia it cannot be identified with it.

Ta Thung and *Thai Phing* found their place in utopia, but not until the nineteenth century, and not until they had been decisively fused with Western thought. The first signs of this were in the Thai-Phing Rebellion of 1851–64, where Christian millenarianism was a prominent feature of the rebel leader Hung Hsiu-ch´uan's religion. *Ta Thung* and *Thai Phing* were given a more clearly utopian framework in the first true Chinese utopia, the *Ta Thung Shu* (Book of the Great Togetherness), written between 1884 and 1913 by Khang Yu-Wei.[30] Khang proposed a return to the principles of primitive Confucianism. But this Wellsian utopia of a world state powered by atomic energy only too clearly revealed how far Western thought and practice had penetrated the Chinese intelligentsia. With its enlightened educational practices, its progressive sexual and racial policies, above all its idolization of science and technology, the *Ta Thung Shu* declared in unmistakable tones that the Chinese utopia was also the Western utopia.

One reason why it is difficult to find utopia in non-Western societies is that they have mostly been dominated by religious systems of thought. It is this that also makes problematic the idea of a Christian utopia. Utopia is a secular variety of social thought. It is a creation of Renaissance humanism. Its practitioners have often been devout Christians – Francis Bacon no less than Thomas More –but what their utopias principally declared was a faith in human reason. In their utopias, whatever the case in their other speculations, they were more concerned with the City of Man than the City of God.

Early and mediaeval Christianity therefore produced no utopia.[31] Some have treated Augustine's fifth-century *City of God* as a utopia. But a work that takes so seriously to heart Christ's saying 'My kingdom is not of this world' can hardly be considered utopian (although it certainly supplied an influential line of thought to the later *anti*-utopia). If this world is no more than 'a dark vestibule leading to the great hall of the next world',[32] how can utopian plans to perfect this world ever be more than damnable presumption? Certainly that seems to have been the general attitude towards utopianism – or what might pass for it – in the Middle Ages, when Augustine's influence was paramount in orthodox circles. The *contemptus mundi*, an attitude frequently encountered in Christianity's history, can only be profoundly discouraging to utopian speculation.

It may nevertheless be the case that Christianity is part of the reason why utopia has developed in the West and nowhere else. This is not so much owing to the Paradise concept – in any case widespread – although undoubtedly Paradise contributed its characteristic tones and imagery to utopia. Nor was it monasticism that was peculiar to the Christian tradition – it is equally strong in Buddhism – although again the example and model of the mediae-val monastery was a powerful influence on utopia (particularly clear in More's *Utopia* and Campanella's *City of the Sun*).

More important is the peculiar strength of millenarianism in Christianity as compared with other religions. The vision of a per-fected order on earth, one that was predestined and therefore not an empty dream, inspired countless radical movements in the West and affected Western thought in innumerable ways. It is impossible to say whether or not utopianism would have arisen without millen-arianism, but it is certain that it contributed immeasurably to the expressive force of utopia. The imagery of the new heaven and the new earth from *Revelations*, elaborated by many later writers, insin-uated itself into the Western utopia. Later the secularization of the millennium in the idea of progress continued to lend utopia a dyna-mism and an emotional force without which its appeal would un-doubtedly have been severely diminished.

But the millennium is not utopia. Its ideal order is predeter-mined. It is brought in by divine intervention. Human agency remains questionably relevant. The millennium is not, as is utopia, a scheme of perfection to be realized – if at all – by conscious rational human action. Although it is in history and not beyond it, it is history as disclosed by faith not by reason. More's Utopians are pagans, as are Campanella's Solarians and – albeit latterly Chris-tianized – the citizens of Bensalem in Bacon's *New Atlantis* (1627). More's Utopia is, as R. W. Chambers reminds us, 'a pagan state founded on Reason and Philosophy'.[33] The implication must be that even devoutly Christian thinkers regarded utopia as an order belonging unambiguously to this world, to be achieved with its materials and by the free agency of its human inhabitants. To Christian thinkers utopia might not be the summit and end of man's destiny; that must be for another world. But so far as this world was concerned it represented the best order that could be achieved by unaided human purpose and design. 'Utopia transcends the given social reality', Moses Finley has said; 'it is not transcendental in a metaphysical sense.'[34]

Utopias of the classical world

If not a Christian origin of utopia, what of a pagan one? The Hellenic inheritance of utopia is less easy to disengage. Of all the older forms that may be considered elements of utopia, the Hellenic ideal city seems the most fitted to be utopia's precursor or progenitor. Thus Olson: 'Utopia as a type arises on Greek cultural soil; it could have arisen nowhere else.' Coupled with this goes a general recognition of the overwhelming importance of Plato in the utopian tradition, so that, whether or not we call Plato a utopian, he is 'the progenitor of the genre'; he 'established the ground plan which governed later utopias.'[35]

The argument against the ancient Greek origins of utopia do not turn primarily, as it does with Christianity, on the issue of transcendentalism. The case indeed might seem to go the other way. For although the ideal-city tradition was rooted in cosmological ideas, usually of a religious kind, the keystone of that cosmology was reason. Man's god-given faculty of reason mediated between the divine order of the cosmos and the ideal order of the city. In Plato's philosophy it was reason that permitted the penetration of reality, the apprehension of the eternal and perfect forms that lay behind the world of appearances. This rational apprehension could lead to the construction – in principle at least – of the perfect order of society. Since the later utopia also took its stand on reason, since in any case the Renaissance humanists who invented the genre were ardent admirers of Plato, it is easy to see why so many commentators choose to regard utopia as primarily Greek in inspiration.

So much might be admitted while still insisting on the originality of More's invention. More, like all later utopians, felt himself inspired and challenged by Plato's *Republic*. It was impossible for him, as for Morris or Wells, to discuss the good society without referring to Plato's ideas on the subject. One might even go so far as to say that the very enterprise of conceiving and describing the best state of the commonwealth was owing to Plato's example in the *Republic* and the *Laws*. But utopia is not just the conception of the good or perfect society. It is a particular and distinctive way of discussing the good society. It has its own form. Moreover it arose at a time when the very idea of what constituted the good society was being transformed. This gave it too a distinctive content. In both these ways the utopia of More's invention distanced itself from the ideal city of the ancient Greek and Roman world.

We are apt to forget, in the frequency with which Classical utopias are invoked, how few are the Classical texts which have any claim to be considered as utopias. Most so-called utopias of antiquity are in the form of Golden Age myths, or stories of fantastic peoples and places, often for satirical purposes. They can also appear as exercises in philosophical analysis. John Ferguson's extensive survey, *Utopias of the Classical World* (1975), starts with the fanciful idealization of the Phaeacians in the *Odyssey* and ends with Augustine's *City of God*. In between pride of place is properly reserved for Plato; but we also have an account of Aristotle's 'best possible society' – partly a critical response to Plato's *Republic* – in the last two books of the *Politics*. Leaving aside the many primitivist evocations, as in Virgil and Ovid, and Roman eulogies of the reigns of various emperors, the other significant utopias are said to be found mainly in the third-century BC Hellenistic literature of the 'imaginary voyage': chiefly Euhemerus's account of the Sacred Isle, and Iambulus's description of his stay in the Islands of the Sun. The latter gains further status as the putative inspiration of Aristonicus's short-lived Heliopolis or Sun State, a supposedly utopian social order founded in a rebellion of slaves and poor peasants in Pergamum in the second century BC.

Ferguson does not attempt to define utopia; and indeed it would be difficult to imagine any concept which could link so heterogeneous a group of writings. They differ moreover not simply in the mix of the manifestly fabulous with the rational and realistic; as texts they offer themselves to us in a perplexing variety of forms. There are playful digressions in moral epics or serious works of history, satires resorting to burlesque and fantasy, stories of adventure and romance, philosophical treatises. The accounts of Euhemerus and Iambulus, generally taken to be the most important of the formal literary utopias of the ancient world, do not appear in their own hand but are known to us only in a garbled form in the first century BC compilation *The Library of History*, by Diodorus Siculus. In any case, they are more like Baron Munchausen stories than the realistic fiction of the utopia.[36] As for Aristonicus's Sun State, not only is virtually nothing known of it but there now seems no foundation to the belief that it was connected to Iambulus's Islands of the Sun.[37]

This really leaves just Plato and mainly his *Republic*. The *Critias*, as we have seen, comes closest to the utopia in form, but it is the merest fragment. In the *Statesman* and the *Laws* Plato deliberately turned away from the best state to the second best, to what might be achievable with the materials to hand in the existing institutions and practices of contemporary societies. This too was Aristotle's pragmatic approach to the good society in the *Politics*. Only the *Republic* comes anywhere near fulfilling the requirements of a utopia: the presentation of an ideal society in all the detail of its private and public life.

To say this is at once to see why the *Republic* is not a true utopia (though it can certainly be held to be a work of utopian theory). It is at most a portrayal of the principles of the ideal state, not an exemplification of those principles in action, in concrete institutions and ways of life. Plato himself admits as much in the *Timaeus*, when Socrates expresses his wish to see the principles of the Republic imaginatively realized and embodied in living and moving men and women. The *Republic*, whatever it is, is clearly no 'speaking picture' utopia.

There is a further and perhaps more serious difficulty. Plato's concern in the *Republic* is not so much the good or just society as the good or just individual. In fact of course his concern is even more abstract: it is the nature of justice itself, the ideal form of which is imperfectly mirrored in the just individual and the just society. But Socrates early decides that the principle of justice can best be considered from the aspect of the just individual. This remains the underlying point of reference throughout the dialogue. In seeking to define the just man, Socrates then suggests that it will be easier to do this if justice is projected on to a larger plane, the plane of the just state: for 'in the larger the quantity of justice is likely to be larger and more easily discernible'. But the promise is made that 'when the State is completed there may be a hope that the object of our search' – the nature of justice in the individual – 'will be more easily discovered.'[38]

Towards the end of the *Republic* Socrates delivers on his promise. He returns to the original concern, justice in the individual soul. The question of the practical realization of the just state is dismissed as irrelevant. The just state has served its purpose. It has shown in a magnified form the composition and harmonious organization of the just soul. In the just individual, as in the just state, reason will

rule, supported by will and in control of appetite (which however
has its due place in the economy of the soul, just as the artisans do in
the economy of the state). Armed with this internal order the just
man can live virtuously in any kind of society. He will be indifferent
to the lure of riches or reputation in the particular society in which
he happens to find himself. The just man need consider only 'the
city which is within him'. When Glaucon suggests that this must
mean that the just man 'will not be a statesman', Socrates retorts:

> By the dog of Egypt, he will! in the city which is his own he certainly
> will, though in the land of his birth perhaps not, unless he have a
> divine call.
>
> [Glaucon]: I understand; you mean that he will be a ruler in the city
> of which we are the founders, and which exists in idea only; for I do
> not believe that there is such a one anywhere on earth?
>
> In heaven, I replied, there is laid up a pattern of it, methinks,
> which he who desires may behold, and beholding, may govern
> himself accordingly. But whether such a one exists, or ever will exist
> in fact, is no matter; for he will live after the manner of that city,
> having nothing to do with any other.[39]

There can, of course, be utopias of the contemplative life, and
other utopias primarily concerned with individual happiness or
fulfilment. This may be said to be the focus of the modern
'eupsychia', the psychological utopias of Wilhelm Reich, Erich
Fromm and Herbert Marcuse. But these are also Marxist or socialist
thinkers. Their visions of individual fulfilment are squarely set
within the context of radically transformed societies even though
their main interest is in the reconstitution of individual psychology.
Utopia is essentially a form of social thought. Its premise is that the
good individual will only be found in the good society. The Greeks
knew this of course – who better? - but in the *Republic* at least Plato
is concerned with a different kind of problem. What he offers in the
Republic is not a sociological treatise in utopian form but a tract for
philosophical contemplation.

The question, again, is not one of the realizability or practicability of utopia. We cannot make this, in any simple form at least, a
criterion of utopian intent. Many later utopias were clearly
unconcerned with it. But Plato's treatment of the ideal society in the
Republic raises a more difficult problem. At one point Socrates, in
full flood on the detailed programme of studies for the Guardians,

laughingly remembers himself and says that he had in the heat of his enthusiasm for the subject forgotten that 'these speculations are only an amusement for our leisure.'[40] We too need to remember that the *Republic*, like all of Plato's work, is a dialogue, that is a form that follows through the logic of an argument often to absurd conclusions, as in the *Symposium*. It is not, despite certain obvious flights of playfulness, that Plato is not serious. It is simply that we do not really know what Plato himself thought, what he intended us to take as his true views on the ideal society or any other matter. In the *Seventh Letter* Plato went out of his way to insist that truth is not something that can be put down in words. Only after strenuous intellectual labour and much conversation about it does truth 'flash upon the soul, like a flame kindled by a leaping spark'. Truth is an experience, not a set of intellectual propositions. Hence, Plato warns his would be disciples, 'no treatise by me concerning it exists or ever will exist.' Indeed owing to the inadequacy of language, 'no intelligent man will ever dare to commit his thoughts to words, still less to words that cannot be changed, as is the case with what is expressed in written characters.'[41]

Such radical scepticism may or may not be applauded. But it is an unlikely basis for a utopia. Utopians are not always clear or explicit about every detail of the good society but they do seem firm in the belief that the good society can be written down, indeed that writing it down is the first necessary step towards its possible realization, in some degree at least. The construction of utopias has been a serious part of social theory ever since More. It has followed on the belief, new at the time, that society is an object amenable to scientific study and to rational reconstruction. Utopia has been one of the strands of that study of society. It has differed in its form from other strands, and its obvious prescriptive intent also marks it off from other more conventional approaches. But it has never ceased to regard itself as a form of critical and constructive social analysis. Plato's questing, dialectical and speculative manner has been enormously influential in many spheres and occasionally it has been imitated by the utopia; but generally the utopia chose other modes to follow.

The Hellenic ideal city, and Plato in particular, had much to contribute to utopia. But it cannot be identified with it. More's *Utopia* launched a different tradition of social thought upon the world. The literary utopia contained possibilities, aesthetic and sociological, not open to the Platonic dialogue, still less to the ruminations of Christian millenarianism and myths of the Golden Age. It could also, owing to its time of arrival in the world, perform its specifically utopian or idealizing function in a new way. It could imagine the new society as an order vastly different from any of the ideal republics of the ancient world. With the invention of utopia, we cross the divide between ancient and modern history. To this, and to the history of utopia itself, we must now turn.

The History of Utopia

The utopian tradition

It has often been argued that to speak of the history of utopia is unhelpful and misleading. Utopia, it is said, is a perennial philosophy, a basic habit of the mind or, even more, the heart which manifests itself at all times and in all places. George Orwell wrote of 'the dream of a just society which seems to haunt the human imagination ineradicably and in all ages'. Arthur Koestler saw utopia as an expression of faith sustained by some of the deepest and most ancient mythical beliefs. 'All utopias are fed from the sources of mythology; the social engineer's blueprints are merely revised editions of the ancient text.'[1] Utopia, in this view, is a timeless and unchanging constant, an *ur*-type or archetype of the human social imagination. It may even be the product of some instinctual 'principle of hope' in the individual human psyche. What could the history of such a thing be other than a dull chronicle of minor changes of style and content?

A view that is not so far removed from this accepts that utopia arose under certain historical conditions. But, once invented, there was no further development to speak of, no history of utopia itself. Those who think that utopia was invented by Plato can speak of it as a more or less unchanging entity stretching over more than two millennia.[2] Those who think that More was the inventor claim more modestly that utopia 'has barely changed in the last four and a half centuries.'[3] There is a basic agreement, though, on the relatively constant and unchanging character of utopia. In one such version, utopia is seen as a particular and distinctive mode of the ideal society that, once adopted, imposes certain well nigh unavoidable constraints on the handling of the subject of the ideal society. Differences of historical time can only marginally affect this basic uniformity of treatment.

> That is why a nineteenth-century utopia like Edward Bellamy's *Looking Backward* shares common features and structures with More's *Utopia* . . . because they made similar assumptions and came to similar conclusions; because they chose a common mode of ideal society.[4]

This determinist form of literary or typological idealism is therefore yet another way of banishing history. A third way, somewhat related, is to treat utopia as a form of thought that is self-consciously ahistorical. The main point here is that utopia expels history from its timeless order of perfection. But this approach also generally has the effect of sealing utopia itself from history, from changes in the society in which it appears. Thus Theodore Olson sees utopianism as 'the search for the good pattern of life in an ahistorical cosmos'. It is committed to 'the notion of a cosmos in which historical development fundamentally adds nothing'. At the same time such utopianism assumes the best pattern of life to be always there, existing in an eternal realm, waiting to be discovered by reason. It may, for various reasons, only be discovered at a certain point in history, but in principle 'it could have been discovered at any prior time'.[5] Utopia not only expels history from its own fictional world; it also presents itself as an eternally existent realm of thought only waiting for its Columbus.

At the other extreme is the radical historicization and contextualization of ideas associated especially with Quentin Skinner. Skinner roundly dismisses the study of 'unit ideas' – the tracing of some grand, essentially persistent, theme over a long period – as influentially practised by Arthur Lovejoy and his disciples. Words – ideas such as utopia, progress, equality – do indeed persist. But their meanings and the intentions of their users can change dramatically over time. Skinner hence advocates 'a history necessarily focused on the various agents who used the idea, and on their varying situations and intentions in using it'. Such an approach leaves no room for the traditional study of the history of an idea, nor indeed for any useful or meaningful concept of it.

> If an historian, for example, who studies the idea of Utopia comes to see that the uses to which the idea has been put are bewilderingly

various, then it would seem little more than a very misleading
fetishism of words to go on trying to make any sort of historical study
out of focusing on the 'idea' of Utopia itself . . . For the persistence
of such expressions tells us nothing reliable at all about the
persistence of the questions which the expressions may have been
used to answer, or the intentions generally of the various writers who
may have used the expression.[6]

This clearly has force, especially in the hands of so powerful an
advocate. But if all it leaves us with is 'a history of the various
statements made with the given expression', we might seem at a loss
to know what to do with some familiar and important facts about
utopia. For in the first place it is clear that writers through the ages
have consciously and deliberately gone back to earlier utopias as
models, as examples of ways of examining and criticizing society
and proposing changes within it. And in the second place, even
where writers have wished to alter the terms of former utopias, to
do new things with utopia as a form, they have shown themselves
acutely conscious of their predecessors. They have gone out of their
way to stress the areas of agreement and disagreement between
themselves and earlier utopias and to indicate any new departures
they might wish to make. In all these ways utopian writers have
proclaimed themselves to be working self-consciously within a
utopian tradition.

There is, it is true, nothing in Skinner's method that would
prevent such a conclusion emerging from a history of utopia, or any
other political concept, in the terms suggested by him.[7] But it seems
fair to say that his method does not encourage such a study, nor does
it lead one to expect such an outcome. All its weight is thrown on to
particular contexts and discrete historical configurations, as more or
less self-contained entities for analysis. Connections and continuities between them may occur, but that is not the principal focus of
investigation. Whereas in the case of utopia at least the striking
thing is not merely the continuity of literary form but the constancy
of themes, the preoccupation with certain characteristic problems
and the continuous argument about the best possible solutions to
them. All this suggests the idea of a tradition.

None of this, on the other hand, should throw us back on the idea
of a timeless structure of thought or some sort of archetype. An
intellectual tradition, like any other, involves both continuity and
change. Clearly something must link the different uses of a concept

to establish that we are analysing a tradition. But that something need be no unchanging essence or core. We are speaking here, in the human sciences at least, of a far looser understanding of concepts and their history. There are certain overlaps of meaning, extensions and refinements of use, criticisms of received opinions, redirections in the possible application of the concept.[8] Writers need not be responding directly to past utterances, nor even to have read many of them. 'Influences' of this kind are not the most important. But they are aware, from the intellectual culture of which they are a part, of a tradition of thinking which takes a certain form, employs certain literary techniques, and is directed to the analysis of certain problems. In engaging with that tradition they involve themselves in a whole history of thought.

Utopia is such a tradition of thought. From the time of More's *Utopia* there has been no century, probably no decade, in which utopias have not been written.[9] Already by the early seventeenth century the word 'utopian', in most of its customary meanings, had become lodged in the major European languages. More's *Utopia* had appeared in its original Latin in Louvain, Paris, Basel, Florence, Cologne and Oxford, and it had been translated into English, French, Italian and German. (In one European language or another it has never been out of print since its first publication.)[10] It had directly inspired three of the most celebrated utopias of early modern times: Anton Francesco Doni's *I Mondi* (1553), Johann Valentin Andreae's *Christianopolis* (1619), and Tommaso Campanella's *City of the Sun* (1623). Their fame in the seventeenth century further spread that of utopia as a new and commanding genre. The same was also true of Robert Burton's *Anatomy of Melancholy* (1621–38), which has been called 'the first proper utopia written in English'. This seventeenth-century classic not merely critically reviewed the utopias of More, Andreae, Campanella and Bacon; it also presented its own utopia, 'a New Atlantis, a poetical commonwealth of mine own', largely indebted to More and Bacon. Francis Bacon's scientific utopia, *New Atlantis* (1627), had indeed appeared during the successive revisions of Burton's book, thus allowing him to add it to the tally of famous utopias available for commentary and criticism. Also available at that time, although Burton chose not to discuss it, was the first of the long line of mocking and satirical anti-utopias, Bishop Hall's *Mundus Alter et Idem* (1605).

Here was established the pattern of the utopian tradition: an elaborate counterpoint of imitation, continuation, disputation, refutation. It is illustrated above all by what happened to More's *Utopia* between the sixteenth and eighteenth centuries. Later, following Newton, the scientific utopias of Campanella and Bacon became the central points of reference, especially in the Enlightenment. This could include ribald treatment, as in Swift's *Gulliver's Travels* (1726). After a mid-nineteenth century hiatus, the utopian form re-emerged to continue the pattern of challenge and response. Edward Bellamy's state-socialist utopia *Looking Backward* (1888) was indignantly repudiated in William Morris's alternative vision of socialism, *News from Nowhere* (1890). Morris was in his turn reproved by H. G. Wells in *A Modern Utopia* (1905), a utopia of science that also harked back to Plato, More and especially Bacon. Wells, as both model and target, himself inspired the anti-utopias of Evgeny Zamyatin (*We*, 1924), Aldous Huxley (*Brave New World*, 1932), and George Orwell (*Nineteen Eighty-Four*, 1949). In 1948 B. F. Skinner gleefully turned the tables on Huxley by employing many of the devices of *Brave New World* in his utopia of 'behavioural engineering', *Walden Two*. The example must have been infectious, for Huxley also later reversed himself. In his utopia *Island* (1962) he attempted to dispel some of the gloom he had created by showing now how *Brave New World* practices could be deployed in a positive way. But *Island's* aesthetic, anarchistic, low technology vision of the good life also strongly recalled William Morris; and it was Morris, rather than Huxley, who became the cult figure in the ecological utopia or 'ecotopia' of the 1970s and 1980s.

Utopia's career has been chequered; but there is no doubting its continuity. It has the tide-like ebb and flow that mark many other long-standing traditions of thought, such as millenarianism. A powerful current in the sixteenth and seventeenth centuries it seemed in the late eighteenth century to lose purpose and direction. In its formal literary form it was for much of the nineteenth century relegated to the margins of Western thought. Utopianism indeed still flourished, but in the guise rather of utopian social theory and utopian communal experiments. Towards the end of the nineteenth century the literary utopia re-emerged in its fully fledged form. Its vigour and popularity stimulated the life of the dystopia or anti-utopia, its *alter ego*. The anti-utopia once again gave utopia, at least in form, a dominant position in the first half of the twentieth century. In the second half of this century it has again seemed to falter; but, with the approach of the end of the second millennium, there are signs of a powerful resurgence.

Utopia and modernity

Utopia, it is clear, has a history; but it is also *in* history. Its view of the good life is affected by the contemporary reality in which it appears. Utopians are not seers of a miraculous kind. They do not enjoy the gift of prophecy. They may anticipate reality but their visions are also constrained by the sort of society in which they are conceived.

Ancient views of the good life were bounded by what seemed the inescapable limits to ancient society. Among these were the necessity of inequality and hierarchy. As Lewis Mumford has said, 'it was easier for . . . Greek utopians to conceive of abolishing marriage or private property than of ridding utopia of slavery, class domination, and war.'[11] All ancient utopias assume the existence of a mass of servile workers who do not normally partake in the good life.

Even with the most radical vision, that of Plato's *Republic*, these limits are apparent. Aristotle complained that Plato had left us almost totally in the dark about 'the mass of the citizens who are not guardians' – in other words, the third estate of farmers and artisans – even though they must make up 'nearly the whole of the citizen body'. He raised the spectre of 'two states in one, and those two states will be opposed to one another – the Guardians being made into something of the nature of an army of occupation, and the farmers, artisans, and others being given the position of ordinary civilians.' Plato, said Aristotle, 'makes one body of persons the permanent rulers of his state', a system which must breed 'discontent and dissension' among that vast majority excluded from power.[12]

But the most serious limitation in the *Republic* relates to its communism. Aristotle was unclear how far the community of property and of wives and children applied to the farmers and artisans, as much as it does to the two classes of guardians, the philosopher-kings and the auxiliaries. Plato in fact is quite specific about this: communism in the ideal state is strictly restricted to the guardians. The farmers own private property and live in private families. They alone cultivate the land. Part of the produce, in the form of 'a fixed rate of pay, enough to meet the expenses of the year and no more', goes to supporting the guardians in return for their discharge of political and military duties. The guardians, like the priestly Brahmins of traditional India, are a 'kept' class, a salaried class of public officials dependent on the productive labour of a host of private smallholders.

There really could be no other arrangement, given Plato's basic conception in the *Republic*. The communism of the guardians is not intended as a principle regulating the life of the community as a whole. Even among the guardians it is not, like modern communism, a communism of producers; it is at most a 'communism of consumption'. The guardians have no land or houses; they live 'encamped' in common barracks, like soldiers. The communism of the guardians has a specific moral purpose, to provide an environment that will 'neither impair their virtue as guardians, nor tempt them to prey upon the other citizens'.[13] It is a communism of asceticism and abnegation. The guardians are there to perform a specific function: to cultivate the knowledge of the ideal and to apply this so far as they can to the imperfect world of men. Nothing must be allowed to distract them from this supreme task – neither the need to earn their daily bread, nor the pleasures and preoccupations of marriage and child rearing. They must remain free of all family entanglements, all temptations that go with the possession of private property. It is this renunciatory purpose that is at the root of their ascetic communism.

> Both the community of property and the community of families . . .
> tend to make them more truly guardians; they will not tear the city in
> pieces by differing about 'mine' and 'not mine'; each man dragging
> any acquisition which he has made into a separate house of his own,
> where he has a separate wife and children and private pleasures and
> pains . . .
>   As they have nothing but their persons which they can call their
> own, suits and complaints will have no existence among them; they
> will be delivered from all those quarrels of which money or children
> or relations are the occasion . . .[14]

'Should they ever acquire homes or lands or moneys of their own', adds Plato, 'they will become housekeepers and husbandmen instead of guardians . . .'[15] It is a remark that reveals as well as anything the gulf that separates the communism of the *Republic* from that of More's *Utopia*.[16] For More's Utopians are *all* house-keepers and husbandmen. Their communism is dedicated to a life of common labour and the homely pleasures of family life. Unlike earlier communisms, this is not the seclusion of the monastery nor the preserve of a contemplative elite. It is a way of life of the whole society. All Utopians share in the daily six hours' labour necessary to produce the food and goods which sustain the community; all share equally in the products of that labour. Work, unlike in the *Republic*, is not something to be left to the private producers while the rulers devote themselves to philosophy and politics. It is central to the life of Utopia. It binds all citizens in a common endeavour and symbolizes the equality that is the central value of Utopian society. 'Let cheerfulness abound with industry', the motto of the nine-teenth-century utopian socialists, might well equally apply to the utilitarian, egalitarian, Epicurean philosophy that underpins the communism of Utopia.

In its universality and fundamental egalitarianism, in its recog-nition of the necessity and dignity of labour, *Utopia* reflects More's Christianity more than his Classicism, his commitment to the equality of souls over and above his admiration for Platonic rationalism. This is what also separates *Utopia* from all previous versions and visions of the good society. More's *Utopia* announced that the modern utopia would be democratic, not hierarchical. The good life would extend to everyone, in all their pursuits – politics, work, family life, leisure and the arts. In doing this, More democratized reason. In Plato's *Republic* the life of reason is available only to the few. In the modern utopia it is open to all. This does not necessarily mean that everyone in utopia practises philosophy. Renaissance utopias, in particular, are marked by a high degree of hierarchy and specialization of tasks. But everyone, whatever their place in the hierarchy, still shares in the good life, because the whole society is the embodiment of reason. There is not, as in the *Republic*, a bifurcation of society into the rational life of the elite and the irrational life of the remainder, the prey of appetite and self-seeking.

More's democratic communism can hardly be said to be rep-resentative of sixteenth-century Europe. More, like Machiavelli at about the same time (*The Prince* was published in 1515), broke through what J. H. Hexter has called the 'fabric of imperatives' of his time: the prevailing norms, values and structure of expectations.[17] So too, though perhaps less radically, did Martin Luther (the Ninety-Five Theses were pinned to the church door at Wittenberg in 1517). Luther's impact was immediate and dramatic; More and Machiavelli had to wait their time. But all three in their different ways pointed to the future: the democratic, rationalist, secular modern world (for what was the Reformation but the harbinger of the secular society?).

Utopia was born with modernity. It was a product of that burst of thought and activity that we call the Renaissance and the Reformation. It blends Hellenic rationalism, the hallmark of Renaissance thought, with the democratizing impulse of Western Christianity that found one outlet in the Protestant Reformation (More's own antagonism to the reformers notwithstanding). The two have indeed been in some kind of tension throughout the history of utopia. The rationalism of utopia has frequently led to a predilection for highly centralized and regulated, not to say regimented, social systems. The democratic and egalitarian strands have countered with utopias that stress decentralized power and local solidarities. The episode in which William Morris's quasi-anarchist *News from Nowhere* was deliberately and self-consciously counterposed to Edward Bellamy's utopia of state socialism, *Looking Backward*, is perhaps the classic example of this two-way tug.

But to say this is simply another way of saying that utopia partakes of the central dilemmas of complex modern societies. It too embodies the often conflicting pulls of the need for order and the desire for freedom, the advantages of centralized large-scale organization and the claims of local autonomy and individual creativity. Utopia, of course, aspires to overcome these contradictions, to show how the circle can be squared. In doing this what it often reveals is the price to be paid for following one or other principle to its logical extreme. This is part of the value of utopia. One of its chief heuristic uses, in fact, is that by the very idealism of its attempt to resolve the dilemmas of modern society it dramatizes them in a vivid and highly effective form. Moreover its own history is a major contribution to the political argument. For not only does utopia generate, as in the Bellamy-Morris case, competing utopias; it also evokes, as a fierce challenge to its whole promise of reconciliation, the grim-faced anti-utopia, its dialectical and equally one-sided counterpart.

Renaissance and Reformation are conventional schoolbook tags for the birth of the modern world. Historians now often dispute this, although this is a game in which we can all join. The changes in utopia in the centuries following More can, if we wish, be connected to evolving phases or stages of modernity, of which the sixteenth century was the first.[18] In any case, whatever the doubts about the Renaissance and the Reformation, there seems no denying the importance of the sixteenth-century European voyages of discovery in the creation of the modern world. And here we encounter another of the formative influences on utopia.

Its immediate impact was literal, in the very literary form of utopia. Starting with More's *Utopia*, the traveller's tale, whether found in the homely guise of the mariner's yarn or the more scholarly form of the reports of missionaries and administrators, quickly established itself as the most popular literary device in the writing of utopias.[19] Time travelling was later added to terrestrial voyaging; later still the travellers in utopian novels were as likely to find their perfect societies on other planets as on their own earth. But as late as James Hilton's *Lost Horizon* (1933) the basic form of the traveller's tale was still thought the most suitable vehicle for conveying utopian ideas to a popular readership. In itself, the traveller's tale to describe 'alternative' societies was at least as old as Herodotus, and was commonly employed by the Hellenistic writers of romances involving fabulous peoples and exotic lands. But the literature of the sixteenth-century voyages of discovery brought a new sobriety and a new realism to the old form. However much embellished by prevailing myths and wish-fulfilling fantasies, there was a factual basis to the stories and reports emanating from the New World that was undeniable. Utopia took much of its force and credibility from its imitation of the voyage literature. It was partly because there were such remarkable utopian descriptions in the accounts of their travels given by Christopher Columbus, Amerigo Vespucci, Vasco de Balboa and Peter Martyr, that European readers fastened so eagerly upon More's similar though quite fictitious *Utopia*.

The voyages of discovery also had a profound influence on utopia's content. The great sea-going voyages opened up not simply the world to the West but also the West to the world. Although it took time for utopia to become global in its reach, the goal was inherent in the relativizing of culture and the ecumenical spirit that were the ultimate consequence of the European voyages. By the time Wells announced in *A Modern Utopia* (1905) that 'no less than a planet will serve the purpose of a modern Utopia', eighteenth- and nineteenth-century thinkers had already reached that conclusion in general terms, although they did not employ the formal utopia to demonstrate it. 'World-state', they would have agreed with Wells, 'it must be.' Meanwhile in the hands of a Montaigne, a Swift or a Diderot the strange ways of exotic cultures could become the material for biting satires on their own societies. Often these were couched in the form of primitivist utopias. In Montaigne's 'Of Cannibals' (1580), the simple native Indians of North America were presented as utopian exemplars, living uncorrupted lives according to the laws of nature. This was a view found in many of the early traveller's accounts of the New World peoples. Diderot also, in his *Supplement to Bougainville's Voyage* (written 1772), had Louis Antoine Bougainville's own widely read account of his voyage to Oceania to draw upon. The portrait of the Tahitians, who know neither government nor laws and live in a state of blissful innocence, is, however, altogether Diderot's own.

Science, history, progress

More's *Utopia* showed its modernity in its democratic spirit. But there was little place in it for science, the other trademark of the modern world. His utopia, like most of the ideal cities of the ancient world, is technologically static and economically bounded. Work in moderation is regarded as beneficial to the mind and body, besides being socially valuable. There is no interest in reducing it, nor in making it more productive. So long as basic or 'natural' needs are satisfied, Utopians have no desire to increase their wealth. They are stern with the idea of artificially multiplying wants – the product, as they see it, of insecurity and vanity. For them the real happiness of life consists in the cultivation of the mind and spirit.

Few utopians have ever disputed this. It is difficult to find a utopia (as opposed to a popular Cockaygne) which celebrates the acquisition of material wealth as such. But there can be a real distinction in the nature and purpose of mental cultivation. For More these were supremely ethical and philosophical. Here he was entirely at one with Plato. For many later sixteenth- and seventeenth-century utopians the cultivation and extension of knowledge of the natural world became the central and most exciting task of mental activity. Not that this excluded ethics and religion. That would indeed have been surprising, given that many of the most famous utopias were written by priests and monks, such as Andreae and Campanella. The religious purpose remained dominant in virtually every utopia written up to the end of the seventeenth century. The goal was summed up in the title of Andreae's utopia: *Christianopolis*, the ideal Christian commonwealth. Science was to be cultivated as the means both to a better knowledge of God and his works, and to the creation of a truly Christian society.[20]

The religious motif remained clear and strong in two of the most prominent utopias of the time: Andreae's *Christianopolis* and Campanella's *City of the Sun*. Both put scientific and technical interests at the centre of their utopias; both subordinated them to spiritual ends. The same was also true in principle of the most famous scientific utopia of all time, Francis Bacon's *New Atlantis*. It does not, however, require us to depend on the contemporary charges of atheism to see that in Bacon the scientific enterprise was in danger of becoming an end in itself. Since *New Atlantis* is a mere fragment, and its message not always clear, it has always been open to many interpretations. But to Bacon's immediate followers, the ones who went on to found the Royal Society, and to many at a later date, *New Atlantis* came to spell the opening statement of the scientific credo. The motto of the House of Salomon can still stand as the banner of all later scientific utopias: 'The End of our Foundation is the knowledge of Causes, and secret motions of things; and the enlarging of the bounds of Human Empire, to the effecting of all things possible.'

So in the century after More was science added to utopia. Just as More's egalitarianism broke with the hierarchical pattern of the ancient ideal city, so Baconian science broke through the static character of all ideal societies up to and including More's. From Bacon's time, democracy and science were the implicit or explicit premises of the modern utopia. And just as utopia's egalitarianism warred on occasion with its rationalism, so too did the dynamism of science threaten to press beyond the boundaries of utopia.[21] The scientific utopia wished to exploit to the full the resources of modern science and technology. But scientific advance was never in itself the goal of utopia. Science was always to be put at the service of some ethical or social ideal. This ideal, once realized in the social system of utopia, was not to be upset by the pursuit of science for its own sake.

This was problematic. Pure science knows no end. It has no point of rest or stability. It constantly undermines existing beliefs and practices. Utopia, however open ended it aspires to be, must in principle be bounded. It is the perfect society and its organization is the embodiment of perfection. There is a finality in utopian perfection which is not to be contradicted by the onward, aimless, essentially anarchic march of science. It is this situation that Aldous Huxley so cruelly exposed in his anti-utopian satire on the scientific utopia, *Brave New World*. The brave new world's whole stability rests on the application of science. Science produces the material abundance and patent remedies that ward off discontent and discomfort. It is responsible for the test-tube breeding of the population into functionally specific castes. At the same time it is a threat to social stability. 'Every discovery in pure science is potentially subversive', says the World Controller. He cites the disastrous experiment of developing new labour-saving devices to reduce the working day of the lower castes. The result was social unrest caused by the inability of those castes to make productive use of the increased leisure time. So scientific research in the brave new world is strictly controlled, the publication of its results meticulously censored. The further irony is that this censorship alienates some of the ablest members of the Alpha caste and drives them into rebellion.

It is unlikely that it was this perception of the threat of science, at least as here formulated, that was responsible for the slow incorporation of science in utopia in the century after Bacon. Partly this was due to the overriding preoccupation with religion in most utopias until 1700. This was true even of those utopias inspired by the fresh impetus to science given by Newton's great work in the closing decades of the century. Science remained subordinated to the task of working out a more convincing religious cosmology, consonant with the new philosophy of the age. Newton in later life himself gave something of a lead, with his preoccupation with the prophecies of Daniel and the Book of Revelation. The same path was indicated in the influential efforts of the Cambridge Platonists, such as Joseph Mede and Thomas Burnet, to reconcile the new science of Bacon and Newton with Christian millenarianism.[22] Utopians such as the Czech Comenius and his English disciples, the circle around Samuel Hartlib, were enthusiastic proponents of the new science; but they were not interested in championing science beyond the confines of the ideal Christian commonwealth that was the principal concern of their 'Pansophias'.[23]

Utopia up to the eighteenth century was dominated by the example of More. The good life was to be lived in a society of equality and fellowship. The seventeenth-century utopia reacted to the emerging individualism of the age by stressing corporate ties and communal responsibilities. The inequalities of private property and the threats to order posed by pride and ambition seemed to be the chief problems needing resolution. The answer was usually found in Morean institutions of communal property and rationally based systems of education. Frank Manuel has aptly described the utopias of these times as 'utopias of calm felicity'.[24] Their aims are peace, virtue, serenity, quiet enjoyment. There is no place in them for the unsettling discoveries of science nor for the unbounded Prometheus of ceaseless economic growth.

So far as the formal literary utopia is concerned, nothing much changed when the centre of utopian thought moved from England to France towards the end of the seventeenth century. Denis Veiras's *History of the Sevarites* (1677–9) and Fenelon's *Télémaque* (1699) are clearly Morean in inspiration, down to such details as the turning of gold into ploughs. Nor was much novelty to be expected from the endless primitivist utopias, such as those of Restif de la Bretonne, written under the influence of Rousseau's *Discourses on the Origins of Inequality* (1755).[25] Swift's *Gulliver's Travels* (1726) stimulated a host of imaginary-voyage utopias in France, although they mostly lacked the wit and bite of Swift's seminal anti-utopian satire (Diderot's *Supplement to Bougainville's Voyage* is probably the best of them). There was a similarly one-sided rendering of Daniel Defoe's *Robinson Crusoe* (1719), which was also eagerly seized upon by the French. In the form of the *robinsonade* it was reworked as a small-scale utopia of arcadian contentment and ideal family life (a trend reinforced by Johann Wyss's rosy *Swiss Family Robinson*, 1813). Frequently the setting for these primitivist utopias was the continent of Australia, which played for the eighteenth-century utopia the role that America had played for the sixteenth and seventeenth centuries (see for instance, Restif de la Bretonne's *La Découverte Australe*, 1781). An early example, and one of the best of the genre, was Gabriel de Foigny's *A New Discovery of*

Terra Incognita Australis (1676). In this charming fantasy the Australians are portrayed as sexless hermaphrodites living in a paradise of natural abundance. They have no private property, no government, no laws and no clothes.[26]

It was nevertheless from eighteenth-century France that there sprang two developments that were radically to transform utopia. The first had to do with the introduction of new themes to utopia, themes dealing with the personal and emotional life of mankind. In Diderot's *Supplement to Bougainville's Voyage*, in the novels of Restif de la Bretonne, and above all in the works of the Marquis de Sade, sexual freedom was put on the agenda of utopia. Sade's *La Philosophie dans le Boudoir* (1795) castigated Christian monogamy as unnatural and hypocritical. All men and all women should be allowed to satisfy their erotic desires to the full. This, he further argued, required the abolition not just of priests but also of kings, and the institution of a secular egalitarian republic. In *The 120 Days of Sodom* (written 1785) he put some of these ideas in the form of a sexual utopia characterized by extravagance and exhausting excess. No later thinker aspired to outdo this. The sexual utopia was given a gentler and more joyful form by Charles Fourier. As a theme for utopia sex remained largely latent – although playing an important part in Morris's *News from Nowhere* – until its revival by the 'Freudo-Marxists' – Reich, Fromm, Marcuse – in the twentieth century. In May 1968 the Paris students incorporated it in their demands for a society free from all repression, personal as well as political.[27]

The second development was more dramatic and more profound. It brought *time* into utopia. Already the conventional spatial boundaries of utopia had been extended by the move to inter-planetary travel. Lucian's *True History* (c. AD 160), a satirical fantasy that was a popular text throughout the Renaissance, had put travellers on the moon and the sun (not to mention in the body of a huge whale). But the early modern utopia, confronted with a still largely unknown earth, was content to find the good society on isolated islands or strange continents. Galileo's telescope and Copernicus's astronomy opened up the heavens to utopia. The general purpose however for the moment remained unchanged. 'Am I doing anything more monstrous [than More or Campanella]', protested Johannes Kepler in defence of his *Dream* (1634), 'if, in a vivid description of the monstrous habits of our age, I transpose the

scene from Earth to Moon for the sake of caution?' The basic
continuity with early utopian themes persisted in Francis Godwin's
The Man in the Moon (1638) and Cyrano de Bergerac's *The Other
World* (1657–62), an exhilarating fantasy of lunar and solar worlds
in the Lucianic mode. The moon or the sun served simply as an
exotic setting, as with More's island, for holding up the satirical
mirror to their own society. The 'planetary romance' (*roman
planétaire*) was in the hands of Jules Verne and H. G. Wells to shape
powerful and original utopias; but in its early form it was still too
excited by the purely technical and scientific aspects of the new
cosmology to show much creativity in its social imagination.[28]

No more imaginative, in its social thinking, was the work that is
by common consent the first utopia couched in the future tense:
Louis Sébastien Mercier's *The Year 2440* (1770). Mercier's utopia is
conventional, even conservative, by the standards of the time.
Technology has advanced somewhat (they are blessed by the
gramophone), education and enlightenment have progressed so far
as to deliver a liberal constitutional state guided by science rather
than religion. But the fundamental departure is to place the triumph
of reason and science firmly in the future. Mercier takes his
epigraph from Leibniz: 'The present is pregnant with the future.'
Just as the idea of extraterrestrial worlds was breaking down the
geographical limits of utopia, so the idea of futurity broke down the
temporal limits of utopia. 'Eutopia', the best place, becomes
'euchronia', the best time. That time – for the moment at least – is
the future. Mercier's censors have burned the history books: the
past is confusing and irrelevant.

It is clear that it was not the formal literary utopia that was
responsible for this turn towards the future. The eighteenth-century
utopia, here as in other respects, followed rather than led eighteenth-century thought. Mercier tapped a current of thought that, in
the second half of the century, was leading Western social theory to
adopt a radically new approach to time and history. The reasons for
this are far from obvious, but they are presumably bound up with
the economic, social and political changes that are symbolized by
the French and Industrial Revolutions. At the level of social theory
the new perspective is most evident in the rise of the idea of
progress, as defined by two celebrated French texts: Turgot's
Discourses on the Successive Progressions of the Human Mind
(1750) and Condorcet's *Sketch for a Historical Picture of the*

Progress of the Human Mind (1793). The idea of progress also finally allowed the full incorporation of science in utopia. For it was clear to nearly all the theorists of progress, Condorcet above all, that the motor of progress was science. Science could be the only acceptable form of thought in modern society, science would be the source of the material abundance that would be the basis of the free and equal society of the future. So too Mercier's utopia directly echoes Bacon: 'Our end is to know the secret causes of each appearance, and to extend the dominion of man . . .'[29]

The socialist utopia

Just as the formal literary utopia did not originate the move to future time, so it was not the main inheritor of that development. In the century or so after the French Revolution there were one or two important utopias taking in the new ideas – Thomas Spence's utopia of agrarian democracy, *The Constitution of Spensonia* (1803); Etienne Cabet's socialist utopia, *Voyage en Icarie* (1840). But in the main the literary utopia went into abeyance, to re-emerge only towards the end of the nineteenth century. If utopianism continued to flourish – and it did – it did so in the form not of the classic literary utopia but of utopian social theory.

Why was this? Firstly, there was an obvious limitation in the whole conception of the classic utopia from More to the eighteenth century. Utopia was not just a perfect but a perfected society. It had eliminated not just the weaknesses and imperfections of existing societies but all activities that might threaten the perfect harmony and equilibrium of its own order. It saw itself as the earthly representation of the timeless realm of truth. Hence the difficulty of absorbing more than a limited amount of science.

The introduction of the dynamic element of time and history threatened to blow utopia's system even further apart. Truth and fulfilment, the culminating point of utopian perfection, now had to be seen as the product of an evolutionary sequence whose future phases could only dimly, if at all, be seen. This seemed to demand of utopia an incompleteness, an open-endedness and fluidity, which in its classic form it was ill equipped to provide. Eventually, in the works especially of Bulwer-Lytton, Butler, Wells and Stapledon, attempts were made to recast utopia in an evolutionary form. Their success, for all their vitality and daring, was only partial, suggesting the formidable difficulties faced by utopia in both accepting change and seeking to contain it.

There was a further reason why the literary utopia, which for long had focused so many of the central political and moral issues of European society, was not the main beneficiary of the new thinking of the age. Thinkers became convinced that progress was not just the law of human nature and human society but that its culminating phases were imminent, in their own time. The dreams of the utopians were on the point of becoming reality. What then was the need for utopias, with their impossibly elaborate schemes of perfection, when the main substance of that perfection was in the process of being delivered by the natural progression of society? To most thinkers at the end of the eighteenth century the urgent task appeared to be not the painting of speaking picture utopias but the elaboration of scientific social theory. Theory could show the true nature of society, past, present and future. It would play a vital part in arming men with the conceptions necessary – as Saint-Simon put it – to 'shift the Earthly Paradise and transport it from the past into the future'.[30]

Utopia in the nineteenth century is therefore largely utopian theory. It appears in the great systems of Henri Saint-Simon, Charles Fourier, Auguste Comte, Herbert Spencer and Karl Marx. Many of these – Marx especially – balked at the term 'utopian' to describe their thought. Utopias were speculative and fanciful; their thinking on the contrary was scientific or positivist. These were handy distinctions for polemical purposes, but they could not disguise the essentially utopian character of the project of nineteenth-century social theory. Comte's 'positive society', guided by a scientific priesthood serving the 'religion of humanity', had the perfection and finality that were the hallmarks of the classic utopia. The 'industrial society' of Saint-Simon and Herbert Spencer similarly suggested that humanity had reached, or was about to, an evolutionary end-point that was at the same time the summit of its progress towards freedom and mastery.

Marx and Engels, it is true, went out of their way to deny that the future socialist or communist society would be a closed or completed system. So much could be admitted, however, without necessarily affecting the perception of the basically utopian quality of their vision of the future socialist society. A society of material abundance, a society which has banished alienation and exploitation, a society in which all men and all women would relate to each other and to nature as artists to their creations: such a conception is in most essential respects utopian (and none the worse for that). The absence of detailed portraits of the future society – 'I do not write recipes for the cookshops of the future' was Marx's contemptuous dismissal of calls for such exercises – no more contradicts this in the Marxist case than in other instances of utopian social theory. Utopia can be expressed sometimes simply in concepts with utopian character-istics – Rousseau's 'general will' community is another familiar example. One of the important innovations of eighteenth- and nineteenth-century thought was precisely to elevate certain con-cepts to utopian status. Not just in utopian theory but also in popular usage 'democracy', 'freedom', 'reason', 'science' and the like could become not merely the constituents of utopian societies but in a real sense themselves utopias.[31]

Some have argued that the decline of the literary utopia at the end of the eighteenth century was tantamount to the decline of utopia itself. Utopia, they say, exists primarily as an object of philosophic contemplation. For More and his successors, as much as for Plato, the ideal state 'is not a future ideal but a hypothetical one, an informing power and not a goal of action'.[32] Utopia is a model of reason or justice, of some other desired quality, which once established in the mind clarifies its standards and values. There is no intention or expectation that such a model will be translated into practice. The point at which men in Western societies consciously devised schemes for the total transformation of society is the point at which utopia ceased to perform a useful function. It gave way therefore to philosophies of history and historical sociologies concerned with the character and future direction of that transform-ation.[33]

Such a view has to come to terms with the very evident revival of the literary utopia at the end of the nineteenth century. Moreover, although it is undoubtedly persuasive in its account of the main function of utopias from the sixteenth to the eighteenth centuries, it is unduly restrictive in its view of nineteenth-century social theory. As we have seen earlier, to limit utopia simply to its form as imaginative fiction is to leave out much thinking that seems to fall squarely within the utopian tradition, and to demand treatment in its terms. Utopia might no longer be largely designed for scholarly contemplation and edification. It might seek now to inspire action, and to be couched in the scientific language thought appropriate to encourage and support that action. But the aim of perfection persists; and its attainability, as with all utopias, remains an ambiguous and hotly disputed matter.

This seems pre-eminently the case with the socialist utopia of the nineteenth century. From Saint-Simon to Marx and Engels, a vision of the future was elaborated which amounts to one of the most imposing creations in the whole utopian canon.[34] Acknowledgement of this came in the most striking way. For, despite the protestations of Marx, Engels and the official socialists, it was the socialist utopia that became the inspiration of the literary utopia when it revived at the end of the nineteenth century. In Bellamy's *Looking Backward*, Morris's *News from Nowhere*, Theodor Hertzka's *Freiland* (1890), and Wells's *A Modern Utopia*, socialism was established as the modern utopia, the only one that could seriously command the attention of writers of utopia. Vigorous disagreement as to its precise nature was certainly possible. That indeed, with the exception of a few primitivist utopias such as W. H. Hudson's *A Crystal Age* (1887), was the substance of much of the utopian writing of the period. But this only showed how far socialism had set the agenda of the modern utopia.

Later developments confirmed this. The power of the socialist utopia was acknowledged in a backhanded sort of way by the anti-utopians who dominated the period form the First World War to the the 1940s. Zamyatin's *We*, Huxley's *Brave New World*, Arthur Koestler's *Darkness at Noon* (1940), and Orwell's *Nineteen Eighty-Four* all took socialism, in one form or another, as the target of their savage indictment. Socialism's pre-eminence was expressed in the fact that when utopia shifted to its negative pole, to the mockery and despair of the anti-utopia, it was socialism that was taken as the only tendency of the modern world that was seriously worth the full force of its attack. For in socialism was embodied the highest hope of the age. The most influential Western intellectuals embraced it; great societies such as the new Soviet Union seemed on the point of realizing it. For those who were appalled by this, the best way of showing the profound dangers involved was to put socialism at the centre of utopias whose horror and sterility would be evident to all. If socialism was the modern utopia, it had also to be the central subject of the modern anti-utopia. (One can go so far as to say that it has been virtually the only subject of the twentieth-century anti-utopia. In that sense socialism created the modern anti-utopia.)

The waning of the socialist utopia in the second half of the twentieth century therefore posed problems not just for utopia but also for anti-utopia. Both saw the disappearance of the hope that had been the source of their vitality, however differently expressed. The one lacked an object to praise and promote; the other the object of its passionate attacks. The creative energy of utopia, in both its positive and negative form, threatened to dissipate altogether. We shall see, in the last chapter, how far this has proved to be the case. But before speculating on the possible demise of utopia, it seems worth considering the movements and practices that utopia may be said to have shaped during those periods in which it was very much alive. What, in other words, is the relation between utopian thought and utopian practice?

The Practice of Utopia

Nowhere as somewhere

The practice of utopia: what can this mean? Utopia is nowhere; how can it become somewhere? What can lead us to regard actual societies as utopia, or to speak of 'utopian communities' and 'utopian experiments' in the real world? What might be the relation between utopia as a concept or a literary device and these actual, practical instances of utopia?

That there might be some connection, however tenuous, is suggested by the fact that utopia itself is often said to be derived from real-life societies. Plato's *Republic*, it has commonly been alleged, is based substantially on the values and practices of contemporary Sparta; more radical models, coming even nearer to Plato's purpose, were also provided by the philosophic Pythagorean communities of southern Italy. For the 'second best' ideal society of the *Laws* there was Crete in addition to Sparta. It has also been argued by several scholars that More took many of the details – and perhaps something of the substance – of his communist *Utopia* from the accounts of the Inca civilization of Peru that were current in the early sixteenth century. The Incas turn up again as the putative source of Edward Bellamy's state-socialist utopia *Looking Backward*.[1]

Then there are certain traditions, practices and institutions that have appeared to suggest values and forms to utopia. Often these are religious. The life of Christ and his disciples, together with the egalitarian and communal order of the primitive church, have been a constant inspiration to utopias, especially those of the sixteenth and seventeenth centuries. This was true of More; and it was especially true of the radical Protestant utopias of the seventeenth century, such as Gerrard Winstanley's *Law of Freedom in a Platform* (1652). For Winstanley and the Diggers it was the spirit, not the letter, of religion that mattered. So with institutions such as the mediaeval church and the the mediaeval monastery: it was the idealized conception that carried the utopian message. The monastery in particular is powerfully present in the utopias of More, Campanella and Andreae; and even Bacon's House of Salomon shows strong traces of it. Bacon's semi-secular homage to the monastery allowed it to reappear in a fully secularized form in the utopian schemes of certain nineteenth-century socialist sects, such as the Saint-Simonians.[2] Religion in general, as the supreme example of a powerful binding force, continued to affect utopian conceptions in a secular world. It is found in Saint-Simon's 'new Christianity', Comte's 'religion of humanity', Bellamy's 'religion of solidarity', and 'the religion of socialism' that was a strong current at the end of the nineteenth century.[3]

The monastery was a model of order, discipline and communal dedication. It was also a place of joy and fellowship, a place where labour and love were seen to complement each other. As such the monastic ideal clearly corresponds to, even if it did not directly inspire, the classic utopian ideal. For the modern utopia the same is true, and for many of the same reasons, of the army. The military, for all its ambivalence, has for the modern utopia often supplied the model of selflessness and community that the older utopia found in the monastery. The idea of an 'industrial army', dedicated to national service, is the central organizing principle of Bellamy's *Looking Backward*. Other socialists, such as Engels, were also attracted to the idea of conceiving the new order as some form of what William James called 'the moral equivalent of war'.[4]

Utopia has also, where it has wished to show that utopian conceptions are not unreal or unrealizable, drawn on the myth or memory of actual historical time. Nowhere was not only somewhere, it was also sometime. Thus many popular seventeenth-century English utopias claimed to be restoring the condition of the happy age of Alfred the Great, before the imposition of 'the Norman yoke'. Writers and painters in the early utopian phases of the French Revolution harked back to the civic virtues of republican Rome. For some late nineteenth-century utopias, such as Morris's *News from Nowhere*, it was 'merrie England' of the Middle Ages that was the inspiration.[5] In none of these cases was the imitation of the past slavish; but it was clearly important to some writers to show that the life they described was not mere invention but based on solid foundations. Men and women had once, not in some mythical Golden Age but in real historical societies, lived the good life; they might do so again if some of the principles of those times could be recovered and embodied in contemporary practices.

If utopia found inspiration in the beliefs and practices of real-life societies, for the dystopia or anti-utopia this can almost be said to be the defining principle of the genre. Swift found most of the material for his anti-utopian *Gulliver's Travels* in the absurd and dangerous ways of Hanoverian England. Samuel Butler similarly merely had to turn the mirror towards his own society, Victorian England, to obtain the precise picture of the bizarre life of the Erewhonians. All the major anti-utopias of the twentieth century have been so dependent on actual contemporary societies as sometimes to run the danger of merely seeming descriptions of them. Zamyatin's *We* and Koestler's *Darkness at Noon* rehearsed and projected the forms and thought structures of the new Soviet society. George Orwell's *Animal Farm* and *Nineteen Eighty-Four* similarly drew on the theory and practice of the Soviet Union; in *Nineteen Eighty-Four* he added for good measure the contemporary experience of Hitler's Germany and Franco's Spain (not to mention Attlee's Britain). In *Brave New World* Aldous Huxley's targets were less clearly focused; but it is clear that the hateful future he depicted there was largely a projection of the United States, seen as the most developed example of mass, mechanical, commercial civilization.[6]

All ideas grow in some sort of social context. Utopian ideas are no exception. So the relation of utopian thought to actual practices, past or present, is hardly surprising. But equally it is clear that as soon as we examine any utopia carefully its departure from known forms is as significant as its dependence on them. Nothing in the ancient Greek world actually resembled the *Republic* in any but the most superficial way. More's *Utopia* may share with Inca civilization the absence of money and of private property in land but in almost every other way – including its informing ethos – it is as different from it as the earth from the moon. Orwell in *Nineteen Eighty-Four* certainly drew on the practices of Stalinism and Nazism; but what he portrayed in his novel was a totalitarian world of such relentless brutality and terror that many have doubted whether he really intended at all to offer a realistic portrait of a functioning society.

Utopia and anti-utopia borrow many concrete details from the real world (the newly developed department store is effectively utilized by Bellamy; Orwell was similarly creative with the new technology of television). They may even get their inspiration from unusual or striking developments in their world, as More was stimulated by the voyages of discovery and Zamyatin by the Russian Revolution of 1917. But what they in fact are, are worlds lifted by the imagination to impossible heights, worlds where real beliefs and practices appear in a context that transforms their meaning and significance. When during the interrogation scene in *Nineteen Eighty-Four* O'Brien raves to Winston, 'we make the laws of nature', 'we control life at all its levels',[7] Orwell no doubt has in mind the standard Marxist belief that objectivity is a bourgeois prejudice, that all reality is ideological. But in O'Brien he has carried that belief to lunatic lengths, just as the whole political framework of *Nineteen Eighty-Four* is, for satirical and critical purposes, a fantastic and unreal extension of the politics of contemporary states (and not just of the Nazi or Stalinist state). *Nineteen Eighty-Four* can no more be reduced to Stalinism or Nazism than, say, Mahler's music to birdsong, despite the obvious influences in both cases. Whatever the somewhere or sometime of utopia may be, they are no more than distant echoes in its imaginary world, the land that is nowhere.

Thought and practice

If this is true of the origins of utopia it is equally likely to be true of what are held to be the effects or consequences of utopia, at least in the immediate sense. Utopia, it has often been said, has had a direct effect on the practice of the real world. There are some famous examples, though their meaning is ambiguous. Plato attempted to make a philosopher-king, *Republic*-style, out of the young tyrant Dionysius of Syracuse. He himself was the best reporter of the disastrous results of the experiment.[8] In the middle of the sixteenth century a Spanish humanist, Vasco de Quiroga, put into effect a (short-lived) constitution modelled on More's *Utopia* in the Sante Fe area of New Spain in North America. Slightly later the leader of the first English colonial expedition to America, Sir Humfrey Gilbert, carried a copy of More's book with him, and an attempt was made – equally short lived – to establish the first English settlements there along Utopian lines.[9] Over two centuries later it was a reading of More's *Utopia* that converted the Frenchman Etienne Cabet to communism, and led to the writing of his *Voyage en Icarie* (1840). This popular communist utopia in turn stimulated not just a social movement in France, but also the foundation of Icarian communities in the United States.[10]

Two seventeenth-century English utopias provide some of the best documented examples of the practical impact of utopias. Bacon's *New Atlantis* has been called 'an action program'.[11] Bacon evidently expected the practical fulfilment of his utopia of organized science. His many disciples kept alive that hope and worked actively for its realization. The influence may have been indirect rather than direct, but certainly the *New Atlantis* can be seen as a stimulus to the eventual foundation of the Royal Society of London in 1662. As if in some recognition of this the Society adopted the motto of the House of Salomon.[12]

An even more remarkable case is that of James Harrington's *Oceana* (1656). Here we can see both the practical origins and the practical effects of utopia. Harrington was deeply impressed by the equity and stability of the contemporary Venetian Republic, which he had observed and studied at first hand. His republican utopia incorporated devices from the Venetian constitution, although Harrington considerably broadened the social base. In essence he devised a constitution for a property-owning democracy. Its principle was a separation of powers within the state, with elaborate checks and balances to prevent the concentration of power in any one part. Harrington hoped thereby to avoid the excesses both of oligarchy and of democracy.

In this form Harrington's ideal republic was astonishingly influential. It generated a fierce controversy in the last years of the English Commonwealth and led to the formation of a Harringtonian party in Parliament. Neglected in England after the Restoration, it could still stir the normally sceptical David Hume to say in 1754 that 'the *Oceana* is the only valuable model of a commonwealth, that has yet been offered to the public.'[13] But it was in the revolutionary societies of eighteenth-century America and France that Harrington's utopia had the deepest and most consequential impact. The constitution of Massachusetts contained so many ideas drawn from it that there was at one time a formal proposal that the name of the state should be changed to Oceana. Harringtonian ideas also powerfully influenced the original state constitutions of Carolina, Pennsylvania and New Jersey. More impressive still, the shape of the constitution of the United States itself, with its two-chamber Congress and powerful Supreme Court, has been attributed to the influence of *Oceana* through the person of John Adams, a fervent disciple of Harrington's.[14]

Emmanuel Joseph Sieyès, author of the revolutionary tract, *What is the Third Estate?*, was another enthusiastic Harringtonian. In the 1790s, as the French Revolution proceeded on its stormy way, he became increasingly convinced of the value of *Oceana's* scheme of mixed government. His constitutional plan of 1799, with its principle of 'confidence from below, authority from above', followed Harrington closely both in the spirit and the letter. A modified version of Sieyès's constitution was adopted by the Napoleonic Consulate of 1800.[15]

Harrington's *Oceana* is a utopia by the merest fig-leaf of literary contrivance; in most important respects it belongs to the genre of model constitutions that was popular in the English Civil War and later in America and France. Hence its undoubted influence can only cautiously be adduced as evidence of utopia's contribution to social practice. Nevertheless, the examples of *Oceana*, *New Atlantis* and *Voyage en Icarie* make it clear that it is certainly not fanciful or absurd to speak of utopia in these terms. Other well known examples, such as the Walden communities developed under the inspiration of Skinner's *Walden Two*,[16] further confirm this.

But even the most superficial inspection of these and other cases rapidly reveals how frail is the connection between utopia and its practical off-shoots. The New World experiments stimulated by More's *Utopia* failed with embarrassing speed. They were in any case the palest imitation of Utopian arrangements. *New Atlantis* certainly played a part in the movement to establish a scientific institute in England; but every historian of the Royal Society has pointed out that the central feature of the House of Salomon – as an organization of working scientists dedicated to collaborative research – was conspicuously absent in the Royal Society, which possessed neither laboratories, nor buildings, nor funds, and could promote research only by 'honorary means'. *Oceana* may have had

some real influence on American constitutionalism; but in France
Napoleon briskly rewrote Sieyès's Harringtonian constitution,
ensuring that the First Consul acquired a degree of executive power
wholly at variance with Harrington's conception.

Elsewhere in France and America utopia failed to deliver
tangible, practical results. The Icarians in France could never find
the means to try out their ideas in their homeland; but transferred,
under Cabet's own urging, to America, Icarianism proved only a
little less impracticable there. The Icarian communities in Nauvoo,
Cheltenham and Corning never implemented more than a tiny
fraction of the communist programme of *Voyage en Icarie*; for most
of their time they lived a most unutopian existence marked by
dissension, disease and physical and financial hardship. The more
worldly members of the Walden communities such as Twin Oaks in
Virginia have on the whole managed to avoid such trials; but mainly
by departing as often as they see fit from the pure principles of
Skinnerian 'behavioural engineering'.

It is obvious that, in the account so far, we are dealing with a very
literal and narrowly conceived view of the relation of thought to
practice. We are looking for a direct connection between the expressions of the social or literary imagination and the practical life of
society. Most philosophically minded readers will already have been
wondering how soon the author intends to point to the shallowness of
this approach. They are of course right. Thought bears no such
simple relationship to reality, neither in its origins nor in its effects.
Social thought or theory has its own forms and logic; so too social
practice. Practice gives rise to theory, which in its development then
operates in a more or less autonomous sphere of human activity, the
realm of the mind or the imagination. So, too, theory affects practice;
but practice also has its own sphere, a sphere where the pure or 'ideal'
logic of thought must have an uncomfortable existence and must
frequently give way to other more legitimate claims.

These bald statements may not be much of an advance on the
position they criticize.[17] The oppositions they set up are too simple.
All thought is shot through with practical elements; there is,
likewise, no practice that is theory free, not governed by some sort
of understanding that is essentially theoretical. It may even, as in
some Marxist concepts of praxis, be better to think of 'thought' and
'practice' not as in any way opposed to each other but as
abstractions from a unified human activity.

Nevertheless there are times when it is important to make distinctions and divisions within the general realm of human activity. Theory and practice are one such set of distinctions. They accordingly demand distinct treatments. We should not look for or expect any precise fit or correspondence between them. So in the case of utopia. We must examine utopian thought and utopian practice with an eye to their different qualities, as much as to their possible overlap and influence on one another. They are aiming at different things and their success must be measured by their respective aims, not by some presumed unity of endeavour.

The Manuels propose, not altogether seriously, a science that distinguishes between 'theoretical utopistics' and 'applied utopistics'. This postulates the sharpest possible divide between utopian thought and utopian practice.[18] Yona Friedman by contrast has no doubt that utopias are written to be realized and he offers a checklist of conditions for their realization. These then become the criteria for judging the realizability of any utopia.[19] Others have fallen back on various halfway positions, as in Goodwin and Taylor's view of the partial realizability of utopias. Utopias, they say, may be realized 'in principle or in spirit' rather than in detail or *in toto*. Also key aspects of utopia may find their partial embodiment in practice. The Christian utopia has been partially realized in institutions such as the church and the monastery; the socialist utopia has found some partial embodiment in the planning and welfare institutions of most contemporary Western states (whether also in the communist states of Eastern Europe is a moot point). Many contemporary communes, in Europe and North America, also find not just inspiration but much practical guidance in the utopian scheme of Fourier and Owen. Work, family life, the relations between men and women and parents and children, education and the arts, all, it can plausibly be claimed, have been deeply affected at various times and in various places by utopias or utopian thought.[20]

Then there is the idea of what have been called 'practical utopias'. This refers to 'actually existing anticipatory forms of institutions or social orders at a time when their form has not yet crystallized'. Certain practices, in other words, can be seen as radical anticipations of the future, new creations marking out a 'not previously existent social space'. The suggestion is that such practical utopias are often the model for the formal literary utopias of the theorists. An example is Tycho Brahe's famous research community at

Uraniborg on the Danish island of Hven. This late sixteenth-century concentration of scientific research, the first of its kind in the world, achieved Europe-wide fame. It is the 'material', practical inspiration, so the argument goes, for the imaginary utopias of science of Campanella, Andreae and Bacon. 'Before Bacon's imagined house of knowledge production which gave a preview of the Royal Society, we have Tycho Brahe's Uraniborg, a daring utopian experiment . . .'[21]

This, then, gives the sequence first utopian practice, then utopian thought, followed often by further utopian practices that institutionalize various aspects of the first two modes. There is much that is attractive in this. In a broad sense it may well fit such famous examples as Plato's *Republic*, which was partly modelled on the 'practical utopia' of the Pythagorean communities and in its turn, through Plato's pupils at the Academy, influenced constitution making throughout the ancient world. It can also, in an even more general way, be applied to More's *Utopia*, inspired by the practical utopia of Christian communities at various times and becoming one of the principal sources of communist experiments in the modern world.

These examples suggest something of the limits as well as the possibility of establishing some determinate connection between utopian thought and utopian practice. The links are vague and general. It is difficult to demonstrate them. They seem at times no more than nominal. Often practice departs so far from theory as to seem a deliberate mockery of it. The frequent divorce between Christian theory and Christian practice has prompted some of the bitterest reflections in Western thought. The inability of allegedly socialist societies to match anything of the promise of the socialist utopia has likewise produced a literature of denunciation and despair.

We are forced, once again, to consider that utopian thought and utopian practice may be different things, not to be judged by some presumed correspondence between them. They share certainly the ideal of perfection; but the way they conceive that ideal, the manner in which they work it out, follow the different principles of different spheres of human activity. Utopias are not written to be realized, not at any rate in any direct, literal sense. Their ideal of perfection is theoretical; their writers may be quite indifferent to the problems of achieving their goal in practice (which is not the same thing as saying that they are indifferent to the practical value of their utopias). Practical utopians similarly strive to accomplish certain things thought impossible or foolish or naively idealistic by the majority of their fellow men. Success for them may be measured not by how far they match up to the ideal of theory, but by how far they may have shown the possibility of living – even if only for a relatively short time – in ways that refuse the compromises and corruptions generally thought inevitable in human society. 'Thought-experiments', the invention of utopias in the mind and the imagination, are one thing; 'experiments in living', the practice of utopia in small communities or whole societies, are another. Both have their uses, and in either case these can be as much practical as theoretical. But what they teach us will reflect their characteristic differences.

Utopian communities

The 'utility of utopias', their function and relevance in society, will be considered in the next chapter. Here we might ask what is to be learnt from the many experiments in living carried out by the utopian communities of the past two hundred years. Of these the best examples, notable both for their interest as 'patent-office models of the good society' and for the quality of the writing about them, are the more than a hundred American communities formed in the century preceding the American Civil War.[22]

Not all of these American communities can, strictly speaking, be treated as utopian. In fact only one group was inspired by an actual literary utopia: the Icarian communities which, under the leadership of its author Cabet, took *Voyage en Icarie* as their guide. Followers of Owen and Fourier made up the membership of most of the other well known secular communities: New Harmony, Brook Farm, Fruitlands, Skaneateles, Nashoba, the Phalanxes. Neither Owen nor Fourier ever wrote a utopia. For the rest, the communitarian scene was dominated by the religious groups: the Shakers, the Rappites of Harmony, the Moravian Brethren, the Zoar Separatists, the True Inspirationists of Amana. These were not only the oldest but the longest-lasting and by common consent the most successful of the communities. Oneida too, which later evolved into a secular socialist community, achieved its greatest success in its early phase as a community of religious perfectionism, under the leadership of the preacher turned prophet, John Humphrey Noyes.

But the utopian designation of most of these communities is not difficult to justify. Though Owen and Fourier never wrote formal literary utopias, they are the outstanding representatives of utopian social theory. The communities that acknowledged them as prophets were fired by the same zeal to solve the persistent problems of social and individual life. They wished to abolish inequality, to humanize work, to end the crippling effects of conventional family relationships, to free men, women and children from their age-long enthralment to fixed roles and self-destructive practices. 'Democracy was not enough', said the Brook Farmer Charles A. Dana; 'it should be raised up into life and made social.' For the Owenite communities, education was the great panacea. Through education, Owen declared in authentically utopian tones to the communitarians at New Harmony, 'a whole community can become a new people, have their minds born again, and be regenerated from the errors and corruptions which . . . have hitherto everywhere prevailed.'[23]

Owenism was not just utopian; it was also frequently millenarian. Announcing 'the Great Advent of the World', 'the second coming of Christ', Owen in 1834 equated it with the irresistible spread of his socialist philosophy, 'for Truth and Christ are one and the same.' An address of 1833 was even more explicit: 'I therefore now proclaim to the world the commencement, on this day, of the promised millennium, founded on rational principles and consistent practice.'[24]

This conflation of religion and rationalism was widespread in the radical movements of the time; and it is this 'secular millenarianism' that connects the secular communities to religious communitarianism. The most important religious groups – the Shakers, the Rappites, the Oneida Perfectionists – were millenarian. This led them, like the secular utopians, to attempt to live a life of freedom and fellowship, in preparation for Christ's Second Coming (for the Shakers, Christ had already returned, in the female shape of Mother Ann Lee). But, as many observers remarked, the religious groups tempered their millenarian fervour with a hard-headed commitment to the practicalities of communitarian existence. In this they were outstandingly successful. Perhaps their greatest practical contribution was simply to persist, to show that the communitarian ideal could be made to work. It was the 'prosperous religious Communism of the Shakers', John Noyes insisted, that first proved to America and to the world that socialism was not just a paper theory or an empty dream.[25] The young Friedrich Engels concurred: 'The first people in America, and indeed in the world, who brought into realization a society founded on the community of property were the so-called Shakers.'[26]

There were many other indications of the permeability of the boundary between secular and religious utopianism. The Shakers became famous not just for their music and dancing but for the quality of their craftsmanship and their astonishing inventiveness in the field of labour-saving devices. Oneida pioneered techniques of 'mutual criticism' that anticipated many of the later practices of the therapeutic communities. More notoriously, the Perfectionists went in for experimentation in sex and marriage, and in birth control and eugenics, that had to wait another hundred years before being seriously taken up again. The Rappites at Harmony and Economy created model farms and workshops that were the envy of their neighbours. Here and in the Shaker communities no better examples could be found, it was thought, of the practical success of communism. When Robert Owen bought the town and land of Harmony from the Rappites in 1824, he bought not just a prosperous and thriving economic concern but a whole communitarian tradition developed by the religious sects. 'In America alone, the religious socialism of the seventeenth century evolved without a break into the secular socialism of the nineteenth. The communitarian sects were the links in this chain of continuity.'[27]

It has been customary to point to the failure of the utopian communities in America and elsewhere. The religious communities, it is generally admitted, fared well. The Shakers lasted more than 180 years, the Rappites 100, Amana 90, Zoar 81. This is impressive, by any measure. But many of these had ceased to be utopian ventures some time before their end. Both Amana and Oneida abandoned communism and converted themselves into joint-stock cooperative societies. By 1900 the population of the Shaker communities amounted to only 1,000 in all (compared with 6,000 before the Civil War). All the religious communities succumbed to the onslaught of industrialization and urbanization that transformed America at the end of the nineteenth century.

The lives of the secular communities – New Harmony, Brook

Farm, the Fourierist Phalanxes, the Icarian settlements – were briefer by far. Few lasted more than six years, most not more than two, some only a few months. Oneida after it had turned itself into a secular positivist community went into rapid decline. The utopian socialist communities in Britain were no more resilient. The Owenite communities – Orbiston, Ralahine, Queenswood and others – lasted between two and five years, but were often seriously divided well before their formal demise. Equally short lived were the Chartist agrarian communities such as O'Connorville and Charterville, the Ruskinian communal experiments at Barmouth and Totley, and the back-to-the-land colonies, such as Methwold and Mayland, inspired by Henry George and Robert Blatchford.[28]

Princes and other dignitaries made much publicized visits to the communities; but the public attention they attracted seems in inverse relationship to their achievements. Marx and Engels were scathing about what in the *Communist Manifesto* they called 'duodecimo editions of the New Jerusalem . . . which are compelled to appeal to the feelings and purses of the bourgeois'. John Harrison, the historian of Owenism, delivers what has become the received judgement. The record of the communities, he says, is 'a dismal one'. 'Few of them lasted more than two or three years, most of them were plagued by internal strife, and their impact upon society at large appears to have been negligible.'[29]

But what constitutes 'success'? Is it to be measured simply by longevity? Henry Demarest Lloyd, an American socialist of the 1890s, had no doubt that, whatever their life span, the American communities had every reason to be judged successful.

> Only within these communities has there been seen, in the wide boundaries of the United States, a social life where hunger and cold, prostitution, intemperance, poverty, slavery, crime, premature old age and unnecessary mortality, panic and industrial terror have been abolished. If they had done this for only a year, they would have deserved to be called the only successful 'society' on this continent, and some of them are generations old. All this has not been done by saints in heaven, but on earth by average men and women.[30]

Another Labour reformer of these years, referring to the British examples, pointed to another kind of reason for praising the communities. Like Lloyd he did not see the future of socialism in communitarian terms; but 'the fortresses of injustice, inequality, and all evil, are very many and very strong; they must be assailed from many sides.' Whatever the limitations of the communities, they had advanced the cause by the example of their commitment to a different and better way of life.

> At the worst, the development of character and deepening of experience which always results to those who thus boldly take their welfare in their hands, and go out to seek new forms of life under the sun and stars, is a gain.[31]

All utopian communities, Lyman Sargent suggests, have been 'attempts to move from utopia to eutopia: from nowhere to the good place'.[32] As such, and measured by utopian standards, they are inherently doomed to failure, for utopia is a realm of impossible perfection. But that is a long way from saying that they are failures *tout court*, havens merely, as has often been suggested, for the eccentric, the neurotic or those puffed up with spiritual pride.[33] What they are attempting belongs to the sphere of practice, not that of pure thought or theory. They must be judged therefore by their contribution to what Aldous Huxley called 'that most difficult and most important of all the arts – the art of living together in harmony and with benefit for all concerned.'[34] The experimental communities, as he suggests, provide a wealth of experience for us to draw upon. The length of their life is not immaterial – it is after all one way of judging the success of their practices – but it is not and should not be the sole criterion by which their value is assessed. In work, in education, in family relationships, in sexual relationships, in the arts, the communities have experimented with ideas and practices that have often lived on long after the communities themselves have dissolved.

Thus the Owenite communities had nearly all gone by the middle of the nineteenth century; but through disciples such as Owen's son, Robert Dale Owen, and the geologist William Maclure the educational practices of the communities had a far-reaching influence on public education in the developing United States. Also in the United States ex-members of the Owenite communities became members of the anti-slavery, labour and feminist movements.[35] In Britain Owenite communitarianism was especially important, indeed virtually unique, in the prominence it gave to the question of women's role and the relation between men and women in a socialist community. This too fed into the feminist movement of the later part of the century.[36] As for the Fourierist communities, they had a decisive influence on American town planning and the idea of landscape architecture in the second half of the nineteenth century. Through the Fourierist Frederick Law Olmstead New York's Central Park, and similar projects elsewhere, can be seen as the product of the Fourierist community movement of the 1840s.[37]

Again and again, in the 1930s and 1960s as much as in the 1820s and 1840s, when it came to trying out new ideas in education, child rearing, personal development, mental health, environmental planning, industrial production, forms of work, types of technology and sources of energy, men and women have resorted, almost instinctively, to communities. The experience has frequently been painful; but we have it on their own testimony how valuable also these experiments in living have often been. They have learned what might and might not work, what to discard and what to modify. Perhaps even more important, they have learned a lot about themselves, the obstacles to change and growth embedded in their own psyches as members of particular kinds of society. Length of time, whether a few months or a few years, has been relatively unimportant. What has counted is the complexity and intensity of the experience. For those who participate in them, as for those who study and observe them with sympathy, a day in the life of such communities can be a transfiguring experience.[38]

These experiments in living can be of value to any kind of society, at any time. But they seem especially important in the realizing of that larger vision of utopia that has possessed many radicals in the past two centuries. It is this that must make one regret in particular the dismissive attitudes of the official custodians of the socialist utopia. For Marx and Engels and their followers, the communitarian experiments of the utopian socialists were a distracting irrelevance in the development of a working-class movement. In retrospect, and given the experience of communisim in the societies of Eastern Europe, China and elsewhere, this seems a disastrous judgement. Max Weber had pointed to the need to spell out the 'germ-cells' of the organization of the future socialist society, if any confidence were to repose in its promise to bring in a new order. More recently Martin Buber has said that 'the socialist idea points of necessity . . . to the organic construction of a new society out of little societies inwardly bound together by common life and common work, and their associations.'[39] The value of the utopian communities, he suggests, lies precisely in this direction, in indicating the social substance, the 'germ-cells', of the new society. The enterprise of the utopian socialists has been renewed most prominently in this century by the Israeli kibbutzim; but something of the same project of cellular reconstruction has been clear in the many counter-cultural and ecotopian communities that sprang up in the West in the 1960s and 1970s.

Utopian societies

In the Russian Revolution of 1917 the workers, peasants and soldiers spontaneously threw up their 'little societies' in the form of the soviets, or councils. Despite the fact, admitted at the time by Lenin, that the soviets renewed the commune idea so praised by Marx in his account of the Paris Commune of 1871, the soviets were reduced to insignificance by the Bolshevik Party. The attempt was made to construct the socialist utopia without benefit of its 'germ-cells', the soviets. The Union of Soviet Socialist Republics remained an empty promise, concealing the reality of one-party domination by the Communist Party. The results were catastrophic. Seventy years later, under President Mikhail Gorbachev, the experiment was officially called off. The announcement sparked off a wave of anti-communist protest throughout eastern Europe. In Poland, Hungary, East Germany, Czechoslovakia, Bulgaria and Romania popular pressure forced the abdication of Communist Party rule.

Thus in the 1980s ended – or so it seemed – one of the great utopian experiments of modern times. The communities are one kind of practical utopian venture. They are, as it were, utopia on the ground, utopia at the micro-level. But accompanying them for much of the time has been utopia at the macro-level, whole societies that have achieved something like utopian status in the eyes of contemporaries. This often has little to do with the practical accomplishments of these societies, at least on a mundane, day to day level. Much more important is what has been perceived as the peculiar promise of certain societies. They seem to stand for the potential realization of utopia to its fullest extent. Utopia, it appears, might be fulfilled not just in small communities enmeshed in larger, distinctly unutopian societies. Utopia can be writ large as well as small. Whole societies, whole continents even, have at times seemed uniquely embarked on a course of development that would usher in a utopian world of peace and plenty, freedom and fraternity.

We have already noted the utopian status of certain real-life societies. Sparta was one such for some thinkers of the ancient world. Bustling, energetic, democratic Athens could also serve as a very different kind of model. Republican Rome recalled something of the ascetic and communal spirit of Sparta; Imperial Rome became the archetype of the civilizing world-empire. Both were commanding utopian examples for many centuries after the fall of Rome. To sixteenth-century Puritans, Calvin's Geneva was the utopian city, the city of God; seventeenth-century republicans looked to the Venetian Republic for utopian inspiration. In the eighteenth century Geneva once more appeared in a utopian guise as the working model of civic virtue celebrated in Rousseau's *Social Contract*.

All these societies, especially those of Classical antiquity, have continued to feed utopian visions.[40] But since the eighteenth century most of them have increasingly come to seem too small, too parochial, to match the aspirations of the modern world. They are also too limited technologically and economically to deliver the material wealth that is a central premise of the modern utopia. This applies also to the Roman Empire, which can certainly not be accused of parochialism. But the authoritarianism of Rome jars against the democratic pretensions of the modern utopia, thus further disqualifying it as a modern utopian exemplar.

Rome, admittedly, can be and has been frequently resurrected. Most modern empires hark back to it, seeking justification in its 'civilizing mission' which they aspire to recommence. Mussolini's Fascist Roman Empire claimed direct lineal descent; but, even more than its ancestor, its crude authoritarianism, not to mention its obvious nationalism, ruled it out as a model for general imitation. Fascism also offered itself as a utopia of sorts in the form of Hitler's Nazi Empire; but here again its racial exclusiveness even more than its contempt for democracy drastically limited its appeal, even in the Aryan world it ostensibly represented. Somewhat more attractive was the British Empire, especially in its evolution into the Commonwealth of Nations. But here also the element of national self-interest was only too evident, too present, in the justification of empire to permit the British Empire to achieve utopian status.

Indeed we might say that no modern empire has ever been able to attain the degree of universality reached by Rome; hence perhaps why the imperial model has so rarely been able to sustain a utopia in modern times.[41]

It was imperialism also that disqualified revolutionary France. France at the time of its great Revolution certainly seized the imagination of the Western world. During the 1790s republican France was, for many people, virtually identified with the utopian promise of the Enlightenment. It was reason realized, virtue enthroned. But the progression from Republic to Empire, and the attempt to impose the ideals of the Revolution on other peoples by force of arms, speedily diminished France's utopian appeal. As earnestly as the Napoleonic Empire, in its symbolism and much of its discourse, portrayed itself as the heir of Rome, as inexorably it found itself in the role not of liberator but of despot.

It was another revolutionary eighteenth-century society, the new United States of America, that soon established itself as the first of the two great utopian ventures of modern times. This was partly owing to America's own sense of its 'exceptionalism', its providential mission in the world. America was the Promised Land, the place where humanity was destined to find its fulfilment after the bitter years in the wilderness. 'We Americans', wrote Herman Melville in a memorable passage in his novel *White Jacket* (1850), 'are the peculiar, chosen people – the Israel of our time; we bear the ark of the liberties of the world . . . God has predestined, mankind expects, great things of our race; and great things we feel in our souls.'

Nineteenth-century Europeans too, to an impressive degree, endorsed America's special sense of itself. 'America', declared Hegel, '. . . is the land of the future, where in the ages that lie before us, the burden of the World's History shall reveal itself . . . It is a land of desire for all those who are weary of the historical lumber-room of old Europe.'[42] The young Alexis de Tocqueville went there in the 1830s to study the forms of the new democratic society of the future. He was far from uncritical, but his *Democracy in America* (1835–40) pointed to the immense strength and promise of the new republic. More unexpectedly, in view of later developments, European socialists too, such as Marx and Engels, were agreeably struck by the extent of socialistic activity in the United States. America, they frequently declared, would be in the vanguard of the socialist movement; on its 'more favored soil', where 'no medieval ruins bar the way', the working class was developing in consciousness with a speed unmatched in old Europe.[43]

For those utopians, socialist and other, who wished to experiment with radically new forms of life, America always had a special appeal. Nowhere was there a more fitting or congenial environment for their communities than in its wide open spaces. Its own newness encouraged novelty. It was built on the idea of starting the world over again. If America as a nation was not itself utopia, if it remained shackled by the structures of private property and cut-throat competition, America was nevertheless the place where utopias of the most diverse kind could be realized. Outlining his plan for New Harmony to a distinguished gathering of American Congressmen in 1825, Robert Owen discoursed on the suitability and convenience of its situation in the Wabash valley of Indiana. He concluded on a rhapsodic note: 'Here it is, in the heart of the United States . . . that Power which governs and directs the universe and every action of man has arranged circumstances which were far beyond my control, and permits me to commence a new empire of peace and goodwill to men . . .'[44]

To the millions of emigrants who headed for America it was not, as for most European radicals, principally its political freedom that was the great attraction. America was even more, and to a unique degree, the land of abundance and opportunity. If America's democracy seemed to touch on one aspect of the modern utopia, its vast resources and expansive economy seemed equally well calculated to meet the requirements of plenty that was another central aspect. In the myth of 'log cabin to White House' symbolized by Abraham Lincoln, in the 'rags to riches' stories of Horatio Alger, in the whole elaboration of the American Dream, America was portrayed as a utopia of unparalleled wealth and unbounded opportunity whose rewards were open to all individuals of talent and enterprise.

America's fall from grace in the twentieth century has been very evident. But it has by no means entirely lost its utopian appeal. It is still, remarkably, the only country in the world where, given the opportunity to move, virtually every one of its citizens chooses to stay. Whatever the difficulties, whatever their disappointments, it is still in America and nowhere else that they expect their hopes and dreams to be realized. It is America, too, that remains overwhelmingly the preferred choice of emigrants and refugees from other lands. Indeed one region, California, has in the late twentieth century by itself acquired something like utopian status. For the mass of Americans and non-Americans alike it has become the epitome of America's wealth and ease of mobility. With its Silicon Valley technology and a gross domestic product equal to that of most of the major nations of the world, with its freeways and open-air life style, its sea and sunshine, it symbolizes America's still continuing promise as the land of freedom and opportunity.

Even for European intellectuals, proverbially the most scathing about twentieth-century America's materialism and mass culture, America has still not lost its fascination as the country where the future of mankind most clearly reveals itself. Nor is this merely in the spirit of foreboding. Their accounts now certainly tend to be cast in a more ambiguous, more quizzical mode. But for the social philosopher Jean Baudrillard, writing in the 1980s, America is still 'utopia achieved . . . utopia made reality'. It is a society 'built on the idea that is the realization of everything that others have dreamt of – justice, plenty, rule of law, wealth, freedom: it knows this, it believes in it, and in the end, the others have come to believe in it too.'[45]

But it is Baudrillard who also sees America as most truly revealed from the perspective of its great deserts. For it is to him a desert, a flat, contourless society lacking all history and culture. This is indeed the source of a certain iridescent vitality, which appeals to many Old Worlders; but it is also a grotesque emblem of the destiny of the modern world. America in the twentieth century has largely ceased to be utopia. Its own writers and artists have exposed the depths of inequality and exploitation that lie beneath its glittering surface. Its large cities often have the appearance of run down, Third World, shantytowns. Its pre-eminence as the world's greatest economic power has been challenged – by Japan, above all, but also by an increasingly unified Europe. Its military and political might has too often seemed directed to selfish, corrupt and inhuman ends, as in Latin America and South-east Asia.

For many, at home and abroad, America has increasingly shown the face of 'the ugly American'. It has become the image not of utopia but of anti-utopia. It was modern America that provided Aldous Huxley with most of the material for his anti-utopian satire, *Brave New World*. In Ursula Le Guin's *The Dispossessed* (1974) and Marge Piercy's *Women on the Edge of Time* (1976), urban

America is the nightmare of joyless materialism and brutal exploitation that serves as the anti-utopian contrast to their egalitarian, ecotopian utopias. Non-Westerners have echoed this unflattering verdict. America to them stands as the principal agent of a ruthless Western capitalism intent on conquering the world and reshaping it in its own godless image. For many Third World intellectuals, America has become the symbol of all that is worst in the European civilization that imposed its domination on the rest of the world. In the words of Frantz Fanon:

> Two centuries ago, a former European colony decided to catch up with Europe. It succeeded so well that the United States of America became a monster, in which the taints, the sickness and the inhumanity of Europe have grown to appalling dimensions.[46]

If America's utopian image has become heavily tarnished, so too, and more swiftly and completely, has that of the other great utopian experiment of modern times, the Soviet Union. The utopian appeal of the new communist society has been amply documented.[47] Whatever their doubts about particular developments in Russia, to some of the most influential members of the Western intelligentsia there was no doubt that a new civilization was in the making, one that contained the promise of liberation for all. The Soviet Union was utopian theory made reality. It showed the possibility of the socialist utopia. Like America it aimed to catch up and surpass Western Europe in economic and technological development. But unlike America it would do so without the inhumanity of capitalist exploitation. To non-Western countries especially, seeking to throw off the colonial yoke, the Soviet Union offered a model of economic and social development that promised to avoid the consignment of sizable portions of the population to a life of poverty and squalor. It was the first modern society that seemed capable of realizing to the full the modern utopia of freedom and plenty for all.

The disillusionment of the Western intelligentsia has been progressively more intense during the course of the past forty years. Stalinism in the 1930s and 1940s was the principal cause of the first wave of defections. Prominent intellectuals stepped forward one by one to offer their public recantations. Communism was the 'the god that failed'.

> The Soviet Union [said André Gide] has deceived our fondest hopes and shown us tragically in what treacherous quicksand an honest

revolution can founder. The same old capitalist society has been re-established, a new and terrible despotism crushing and exploiting man, with all the abject and servile mentality of serfdom.[48]

With the crushing of the Hungarian Revolution of 1956, and the invasion of Czechoslovakia in 1968, the Soviet Union further alienated erstwhile supporters, in the West and elsewhere. The Brezhnev Doctrine of the 1970s, which reaffirmed the right of the Soviet army to intervene in the affairs of the East European states, was a clear statement of Russian imperialism of the oldest kind. The split with China also showed that communism's internationalism readily gave way when necessary to nationalism, again following an old-fashioned *realpolitik*. From within the communist countries themselves, all the evidence suggested that most of the educated population had lost confidence in the system's ability to work even at the most ordinary levels of competence.

The experiment that began with utopian hopes in 1917 ended in the 1980s with decrepit dictatorships, bankrupt economies and demoralized populations. With the active connivance of the Soviet leadership, itself desperately trying to bring about reform, the peoples of Eastern Europe began to dismantle communist rule. 'In a seemingly irreversible way, the greatest political utopia in history . . . has been completely upturned into its exact opposite.'[49] Like the United States, communist Russia, once utopia, had passed into the realm of anti-utopia.

Is this the end of utopia? With the failure of the great utopian experiments of modern times, with all the other bloody episodes of the twentieth century – world war, fascism, the Holocaust, Hiroshima – what can possibly sustain utopian thought? What are the resources of hope in the late twentieth century? And even if utopia can maintain some sort of existence, what might its functions be? At the beginning, with More, utopia set out an agenda for the modern world. Today, five hundred years later, what are the uses of utopia?

Utopia on the Map of the World

An 'unseemly and subversive' genre[1]

Utopia is sometimes thought of as escapism. It seems to offer the opportunity for light-hearted day dreaming. Who could possibly take exception to so innocent an exercise?

But then why have utopian writers encountered such difficulties? Why have their works often appeared years after their deaths, frequently in bowdlerized and truncated forms? More may have managed to pass his work off as a humanist *jeu d'esprit* but his successors often suffered persecution and imprisonment for their utopian endeavours. Anton Francesco Doni, author of the utopian *I Mondi* (1553), was denounced by the Venetian authorities as a renegade priest and had to leave the city. Campanella was imprisoned and tortured by the Inquisition; his *City of the Sun* was written in prison in Naples in 1602. It was not published until 1623, and then in Latin rather than in the original Italian and in a much revised version that toned down its radicalism.

Harrington's *Oceana* offended first Cromwell, who delivered it into the hands of the censor, and then the Restoration monarchy, which imprisoned Harrington and broke his health. Kepler's *Dream* and Francis Godwin's *The Man in the Moon* were thought sufficiently provocative to justify holding up their publication for many years. Cyrano de Bergerac's *The Other World* had to wait for his death before its publication, when it appeared in a heavily censored and altered form. (It had to wait until the twentieth century for anything like a complete edition.) Veiras's *History of the Sevarites* got him into trouble in London, where it was first published; and it got him into trouble again in Paris, where he continued it as the *Histoire des*

Sevarambes. Foigny's *A New Discovery of Terra Incognita Australis* also incurred the wrath of the magistrates and led the author to a spell in prison, even though he had published the work anonymously and with the name of an imaginary printer on it. Diderot's *Supplement to Bougainville's Voyage*, written in 1772 and circulated in manuscript, was too outspoken for any printer and was not published until 1796, after the Revolution had broken out. Sade was too strong even for the Revolution. His *Philosophie dans le Boudoir* had to be published abroad, in London; he was imprisoned for *La Nouvelle Justine* and then locked up in a madhouse; and his *120 Days of Sodom*, written in 1785, was not published until the present century.

The habitation of the utopian writer has quite commonly been the monastic cell, the asylum, prison. He has had to hide his thoughts behind elaborate literary contrivances and his person behind false names. 'In perhaps no other literature', Glenn Negley has written, 'were so many works published anonymously or under pseudonyms.'[2] The pressure was eased in the nineteenth century when utopia was more or less absorbed and, to some extent, domesticated in the novel, and when censorship was in any case less stringent. But twentieth-century utopian writers could still face difficulties. Zamyatin's *We* was written in Russia in 1920 but the hostility of the Soviet authorities meant that its first publication was in English, in New York in 1924. Zamyatin himself had to go into exile. *We* was not published in Russian until 1952, again in New York; it has never been published in the Soviet Union. Orwell too had problems not just with his 'utopian' *Homage to Catalonia* – it was rejected by his usual left-wing publisher, Gollancz – but even more with his anti-utopian *Animal Farm*, which was rejected by three major English publishers (and one American one) before being published – with some hesitation – by Frederick Warburg.

Establishments of both Right and Left have been equally hostile to utopia. Utopia has been a subversive form: that is perhaps the first point to make in 'mapping' utopia. The very uncertainty over the intention of the author – is this satire? is it wish-fulfilment? is it a call to action? – has provoked authorities to blanket suppression. Better silence it, just in case.

Utopia challenges by supplying alternatives, certainly. It shows what could be. But its most persistent function, the real source of its subversiveness, is as a critical commentary on the arrangements of society. Utopia, that is, is a form of social theory, just as, I have suggested,[3] all social theory aspires to the utopian. Utopia does in its own way what social theory since the Greeks has always tried to do, to give an account of the contemporary – perhaps universal? – predicament and to suggest ways out of it.

Here More, once again, set the pattern. Even if we did not have Book 1 of *Utopia* to indicate his indignation at contemporary practices, the account of Utopia in Book 2 is itself a sufficient condemnation of More's England. At every point, as would have been clear to contemporary readers, the plus of Utopian practice points the finger at the negative of contemporary English and European practice. But More went beyond this. The novelty of his approach was that, unlike the moralists and satirists of his time, he was not content to criticize practices discretely.[4] All the ills of society are traced to a systemic source: the institution of private property. Like Marx after him, More tries to show that 'so long as private property remains, there is no hope at all of effecting a cure and restoring society to good health.' For 'while you try to cure one part, you aggravate the disease in other parts.'[5] It is this which causes Hythloday to reject with such fervour the role of counsellor to the prince. The only honest advice he could give – abolish private property – is so radical that it has no hope of being accepted. All else he could do – go along with the ideas of his fellow advisers, or suggest merely palliatives – would simply 'confirm them in their madness'.[6]

There is one other thing he can do, however. He can tell the story of Utopia. He can describe Utopian institutions. That is to say, he can show the systematic remedy for the systematic evil. This is an alternative practice to counselling princes. Counsel is insufficient because the prince, however good, is just a man and the problem is the system. To show what has to be done to bring about real reform, More-Hythloday has to have recourse to theory. This could take the form of argument from general principles. But More rejects this in favour of theory 'by demonstration'. This is the novelty of *Utopia* – and of utopia as a form of social theory or 'theoretical practice'. More does not merely assert, he shows the systematic interconnectedness of evils and their remedies by portraying a fully realized alternative social order. Only by such an imaginative reordering, he seems to suggest, where discrete problems are shown as resolved in a wholly new way of life, will it be made clear that there can be no tinkering with society but only a radical reconstruction.

It is in this new perspective that utopia is most truly subversive. Most social theory shows the systematic basis of social problems. But its appeal is limited – at least in the eyes of the populace at large – by its reliance on abstract principles. Utopia reverses, in form at least, the a priori, deductive method of most social theory. Its method is commonly rather of the concrete, inductive sort – unfashionable with contemporary philosophers of science but greatly appealing to the common sense of mankind.

Utopia retains throughout its long history the basic form of the narrative of a journey. The traveller in space or time is an explorer who happens upon utopia. He (or, more recently, she) meets its people, usually at first its ordinary people, observes them at work and play, sees their dwellings and their cities. The scenes of ordinary people and ordinary places precede the account given to the traveller of the general principles by which the society is organized. 'It is only later', as Bertrand de Jouvenel points out, 'that he is brought to a center, and the journey thither allows him to observe the landscape before he discovers the main monuments' (Morris's *News from Nowhere* is exemplary in this respect).[7] The traveller is, as we are, the more prepared to accept the validity and desirability of the general principles for having seen with his own eyes its effects in the daily life of its inhabitants. First comes the picture of a happy people in a beautiful and well ordered setting; then comes the lecture on how it all came about, how it works and, by implication, how it might be made to work in the traveller's own society.

Abstract principles may generate intellectual assent among those of a theoretical turn of mind; but for most people seeing is believing. Utopia lends emotional conviction to what may otherwise be no more than an uncertain understanding of general principles. That is why utopia may cause concern to the powers that be, who on other occasions may be prepared to allow or ignore the publication of abstract treatises or discourses in social theory – even where the general principles advocated are in both cases substantially the same. The authorities do not have to worry very much about *Das Kapital*; but *Voyage en Icarie*, or *Looking Backward*, or *News from Nowhere*, are a different matter. So too are simple and forceful utopian tracts such as Robert Owen's *A New View of Society* and Henry George's *Progress and Poverty*. No one denies that these utopian writings won far more converts for socialism than any of Marx's writings.

Against utopia

Utopia may once have enjoyed a privileged and admired status. It was a genre that could at once shock the authorities and at the same time enable the writer to explore some of the most important questions of the social and moral life. In our own century, however, hostility to utopia has been well nigh unremitting. It has been attacked for its basic way of proceeding, for its fundamental assumptions about the nature of humanity and society. It must lead, so the claim goes, to tyranny and totalitarianism.

Utopianism, says Karl Popper, is misplaced rationalism. It believes that all rational political action must be based upon 'a more or less clear and detailed description or blueprint of our ideal state, and also upon a plan or blueprint of the historical path that leads towards this goal'. But ends cannot be determined scientifically; they can only be argued about, among reasonable people, in an attempt to persuade. The utopian method must lead to violence. For since we cannot determine ultimate ends scientifically, the utopian, like all religious believers confronted with other equally uncompromising believers, must attempt to crush all rival visions. He must affirm the absolute rightness of his vision of the ideal state. 'The Utopian engineers must in this way become ominiscient as well as omnipotent.' 'False rationalism is fascinated by the idea of creating huge machines and Utopian social worlds. Bacon's "knowledge is power" and Plato's "rule of the wise" are different expressions of this attitude . . .' We must realize that 'we cannot make heaven on earth'. How much we could achieve by concrete, piecemeal reforms 'if only we could give up dreaming about distant ideals and fighting over our Utopian blue-prints for a new world and a new man'.[8]

For Leszek Kolakowski, too, utopia leads to 'totalitarian coercion'. He is above all concerned that the utopian striving for perfect equality and perfect harmony among humans leads to the suppression of the conflict and diversity that are an inescapable and enriching part of human life.

> A feasible utopian world must presuppose that people have lost their creativity and freedom, that the variety of human life forms and thus the personal life have been destroyed, and that all of mankind has achieved the perfect satisfaction of needs and accepted a perpetual deadly stagnation as its normal condition. Such a world would mark the end of the human race as we know it and as we define it.[9]

Both Popper and Kolakowski were themselves personally in flight from utopia, or what they took to be utopian societies; Popper from the 'Nazi utopia' of inter-war Germany, Kolakowski from the 'socialist utopia' of Eastern Europe. Other anti-utopians, such as Jacob Talmon, were seared by the Holocaust. This reminds us that the anti-utopian attitude is born not simply out of philosophical conviction but equally out of the history of our century. Utopia has been tied to the idea of progress and increasing happiness. It has expressed faith in reason. By contrast the dominating events of the twentieth century seem to make a mockery of those beliefs. Two world wars, mass unemployment, Fascism, Stalinism, the threat of nuclear war – all seem to testify to the continuing power of barbarism and unreason. Latterly, fears of a global catastrophe brought on by environmental destruction have swollen the anti-utopian currents. World society, it has appeared to many, is being prepared not for the utopia of Morris or Wells but the dystopia or anti-utopia of Zamyatin, Huxley and Orwell.

A reasoned pessimism is one thing.[10] The repudiation of utopia on those grounds is quite another. The anti-utopians, overwhelmed by what seem to them the invincible folly and stupidity of mankind, have converted this sentiment into a philosophical and political critique of utopia. In doing this they have made unwarranted and frequently uninformed assumptions about the utopian project. They have generally lumped together all the varieties of utopia as one and the same thing. They have assumed that the literary utopia of More or Morris points in the same direction as the utopian theory of Owen or Marx. It is this that allows Popper to discuss all utopias under the heading of 'blueprints', and to see utopianism as a form of totalitarian planning. No discrimination is made between the intentions of critics and satirists such as More and constructive social theorists such as Saint-Simon. It is indeed difficult to be sure, from the way they discuss the subject, whether Popper or Kolakowski has ever actually read a utopia – as distinct, say, from having read their Plato and Marx. Certainly they show no awareness of the complexity and diversity of utopia as a form and the many different uses to which it has been and can be put.

The contemporary hostility to utopia can partly also be explained by the widespread acceptance of one influential conception of utopia: that owing to Karl Mannheim. The dominance of Mannheim, even today, in theoretical discussions of utopia is somewhat mysterious, and certainly not altogether helpful. Mannheim, ignoring most other concepts of utopia, perversely puts the emphasis on the *realizability* of utopian ideas. Utopias, he says, do indeed transcend the existing social reality. They are 'situationally transcendent ideas'. But that is not to say that they must be stigmatized as unrealizable fantasies. This is the technique and standpoint of the dominant classes, who elaborate their own equally 'reality-transcending' systems of thought in the form of ideologies that stabilize the existing social order. Utopias are rather, in the phrase of Lamartine's, 'premature truths'. Often first elaborated as 'the wish-fantasy of a single individual', they later become incorporated in the programmatic demands of socially subordinate groups, whose aspirations the utopian writers 'unconsciously' and, as it were, prematurely participate in.

Utopias may indeed sometimes contain unreal or exaggerated hopes and expectations. Nevertheless, contends Mannheim, they are properly to be regarded as expressions of those systems of thought which merely anticipate reality, rather than deny it. They are destined, by the force of historical development, to be realized in some future state of society, usually by hitherto suppressed groups. Liberalism and socialism are treated as utopian systems of thought of this kind – and even conservatism, Mannheim argues, can become militantly utopian for hitherto dominant groups pushed aside by the march of history. Hence Mannheim can declare that ideas are utopian 'if they inspire collective activity which aims to change social reality to conform with their goals . . .'[11] Such goals transcend reality but in an inherently and ultimately realizable direction.

Mannheim's determinist and historicist conception of utopia has been gratefully seized upon by the enemies of utopia. He himself in the 1940s and 1950s symbolized for many thinkers the utopian as the designer of blueprints, the rationalist with unbounded faith in 'the plan'. Works such as *Man and Society in an Age of Reconstruction* (1940) urged the necessity of systematic planning if the world were not to relapse into pre-war anarchy. Hence Mannheim's defence of utopia could be seen, and attacked, as a plea for totalitarian planning.

More damagingly in the long run Mannheim supplied weapons to the anti-utopians by his insistence that utopia must be linked to the progressive realization of social philosophies. The utopian project, in this view, was esssentially constituted by the realization of the emergent 'future-directed' tendencies of the age, struggling to find expression against the opposition of established elites. Applied to the most recent period, this suggested that the constituents of the modern utopia were the egalitarian, levelling and collectivist ideals of the age. It was here, too, that planning came in, as the historically intimated utopian means. That these were the essential features of the modern utopia was shown not merely by their presence in most of the progressive social philosophies of the era but, even more, by the fact of their partial realization in the most advanced social experiments of the time. In such phenomena as Roosevelt's New Deal and the collectivized, planned economy of the Soviet Union Mannheim found the evidence of the incipient victory of the contemporary utopia.

This was precisely the nightmare of the anti-utopians. The burden of the anti-utopian critique was not that utopia was impossible, the irresponsible fantasy of shallow optimists: quite the contrary. What appalled them was that the modern utopia was only too possible, that, as Mannheim and others were showing, it was indeed in the process of being realized. The modern utopia of science, reason and democracy was becoming the modern world. But far from liberating humanity and adding to its well-being and happiness, the realization of utopia was bringing in a world of unprecedented servility and sterility, a world where old forms of tyranny were returning in the new guise of mass democratic politics and benevolent state planning. And if so, the less utopian the world, the better. The essence of the case against utopia was put by Nicholas Berdyaev, in a passage which Aldous Huxley chose as the epigraph to his *Brave New World*:

> Utopias appear far more realizable than we had previously ever thought. And we now find ourselves faced with a question that is agonizing in a quite different way: How can we avoid their definitive realization? . . . Utopias are realizable. Life marches towards utopias. And perhaps a new age is already beginning, an age in which the intellectuals and the cultivated classes will dream of ways of avoiding utopias, and of returning to a society that is not utopian, that is less 'perfect' and more free.[12]

'Isn't it time', mused the Russian writer Nadezhda Mandelstam,

> we paused to wonder why the nineteenth century, with its glorification of humanism, freedom, and the rights of man, led straight to

the twentieth, which has not only surpassed all previous ages in its crimes against humanity but has managed, into the bargain, to prepare the means for total destruction of life on earth?[13]

Utopia, the nineteenth-century ideal, had prepared the way for anti-utopia, the reality of the twentieth-century world. And that, argued Kolakowski, was because utopia had offered itself as a practicable, political goal. It wishes to go beyond 'the dream of perfection' and become the living reality:

> A utopian vision, once it is translated into political idiom, becomes mendacious or self-contradictory; it provides new names for old injustice . . . Utopias . . . have become ideologically poisonous to the extent that their advocates managed to convince themselves that they had discovered a genuine technology of apocalypse, a technical device to force the door of paradise.[14]

The revolutionary socialist utopia is regarded by practically all anti-utopians as the main carrier in modern times of this ideological poison. The traditional Marxist antipathy to utopianism has been repaid by a bourgeois antipathy to Marxism as utopia. The attempt to realize the socialist utopia has produced a prison-house, and must always do so. The Soviet Union is the outstanding example of this. So argued Arthur Koestler in his brilliant anti-utopian novel, *Darkness at Noon* (1940). And just as the experience of Stalinism stimulated and reinforced this conviction, leading many Western intellectuals in the 1940s and 1950s to renounce the socialist utopia, so the apparent collapse of communism in Eastern Europe in the 1980s has appeared to many to mark the final end of utopia itself.

The modern utopia is the socialist utopia. So long as there were societies that, whatever their practice, still held up socialism as the supreme value and ultimate goal, the socialist utopia could retain sympathy and support. Western socialists were unsparing in their criticism of East European states, but the existence of societies committed to some sort of socialism undoubtedly strengthened the credibility of the socialist utopia. Once, however, those societies themselves renounced socialism, once their own populations revealed in unmistakable form their contempt for it, nothing was left to sustain the socialist utopia. And the socialist utopia had become equated, in both East and West, with utopia *tout court*. Their fates were seen as inseparably linked. Everywhere, therefore, as the political systems of Eastern Europe crumbled in the extraordinary months of late 1989 and early 1990 (and in the wake of the bloody massacre of Tiananmen Square in Peking in June 1989), voices could be heard pronouncing the death of utopia. The loudest voices were indeed heard in Eastern Europe itself, from the mouths of writers and intellectuals such as the Czech playwright Vaclav Havel, newly elected president of post-communist Czechoslovakia. At best, it seemed, socialist societies could still present the image of anti-utopia; but with the disintegration of the socialist system utopia itself, nearly half a millennium after its invention, was widely proclaimed as ending in bankruptcy.[15]

The uses of utopia

In one of the noblest statements on utopianism, Oscar Wilde wrote:

> A map of the world that does not include Utopia is not worth even glancing at, for it leaves out the country at which Humanity is always landing. And when Humanity lands there, it looks out, and, seeing a better country, sets sail. Progress is the realization of Utopias.[16]

The very familiarity of this utterance has blinded us to its ambiguity. (It occurs, as it happens, at the end of a passage where Wilde is rhapsodizing on a future society dedicated to art and beauty.) Is it to be taken literally – that is, as a call to action, to the practical realization of utopias as the mode of progress? If so, it summons up the worst fears of the anti-utopians and provokes the strictures on utopianism whose force we cannot ignore. The attempt to realize utopias as a political project is fraught with danger. It is, at best, likely to bring about a society bearing only the slightest resemblance to the utopian conception and that in what may be its most superficial features. At worst it will create the opposite of utopia, an anti-utopia of authoritarian regimentation. This has been the experience of all so-called utopian communities and utopian societies, from the American communities of the nineteenth century to the socialist societies of the twentieth.

Utopian conceptions are indispensable to politics, and to progress; without them politics is a soulless void, a mere instrumentality without purpose or vision. But this is quite different from treating utopias as blueprints for action. It is precisely in taking them as such that the anti-utopians are able to score their points. It is the concept of utopia as blueprint that has discredited the socialist utopia and made the apparent bankruptcy of socialist experiments tantamount to the bankruptcy of utopia itself. This is the long arm of the Mannheimian concept of utopias as realizable social projects. It also echoes some of the more fanciful hopes of utopian social theorists such as Owen and Fourier.

For utopians also to engage in this narrowing reductionism is to deny the richness and multiformity of the utopian inheritance. Utopias may contribute to progress in ways other than by the design of political programmes (and this is surely Wilde's own meaning, and example). Its relation to social reality is complex and mediated by many modes and levels. As a literary genre its characteristic stance is in fact a mixture of remote distance from, and fierce familiarity with, the real world of politics and society. This gives it its distinctive hybrid quality, aptly described as 'tragi-comic'.[17]

The utopian writer lives in two worlds. His is correspondingly a double vision. He looks down from utopian heights with a sometimes exasperated or pitying mien but more often with comic relish for the follies and vanities of his own world. He looks up from his own world with a tragic sense of the unattainability of the ideal. The utopia he constructs in his imagination is a perfect world, shot through with reminders of the stubbornly flawed world he inhabits outside his imagination, in his own society. But there is no overriding sense that the one world must, or could, be made to conform to the other. Utopia cannot become eutopia, not, at least, without the great amount of reinterpretation and reassembly necessary to the passage from theoretical ideal to practice. More played with the idea, in some of his letters to his humanist friends and in the Utopian poem he appended to *Utopia*. But the work as it stands gives little support for the view that More seriously thought that Tudor England could become Utopia. The balance is perhaps most perfectly maintained in Swift's *Gulliver's Travels*, where the tragi-comic note is sustained throughout, and where the two worlds are made absurdly remote from, even though they mirror, one another. In more recent literary utopias, where the influence of modern social theory is especially heavy, the pull of eutopia has been stronger. Such is the case, for instance, with Bellamy's *Looking Backward* and Skinner's *Walden Two*. But the high tension between the ideal and the real, which characterizes the literary utopia at its best, is still to be found powerfully present in Wells's *A*

Modern Utopia – despite its reputation – and, above all, Morris's *News from Nowhere*.

As with the literary utopia, so – although more ambivalently – with utopian social theory. The works of Saint-Simon, Owen, Fourier, Marx and Engels, contain many practical recommendations. But they also contain a vision of an ideal future society – not to mention an ideal revolution – that can perhaps best be seen as a critical standard by which to judge contemporary society. Its actual attainability remains an open question, certainly a problematic one. But that is not to impugn its utility. The critical function is as valuable as the constructive one.

The socialist utopia is a case in point. Zygmunt Bauman has persuasively suggested that we treat socialism as 'the counter-culture of capitalism' and, more broadly, as the counter-culture of modern society.[18] It is an 'active utopia' whose terms clarify the main intent and promise of modern society. Socialism takes the slogan 'liberty, equality and fraternity' and shows what would need to be done to make these ideals a reality not just for the few but for the great mass of society. It does this by constructing an alternative society in which those ideals have been fully realized. But their realization takes the form of a utopian projection. It is not necessarily intended that such a utopia should be realizable in practice, certainly not in that form or to that extent. Or perhaps it is more accurate to say that it is not necessary to treat the socialist utopia as if it aims at complete realization. It performs its 'counter-cultural' or utopian role adequately by establishing a comprehensive, critical perspective on modern society.

> Like all counter-cultures, modern socialism performed a triple function in relation to the society it opposed and serviced: it exposed the lie that the achieved state of society was the fulfilment of its promise; it resisted the suppression or concealment of the possibility to implement the promise better; and it pressed the society towards such better implementation of its potential . . . By keeping that society constantly on the move through critique or encouragement, and pointing to new, hitherto-unexplored options, it kept the modern promise of a better, richer, happier society alive.[19]

The predicament of socialism in Eastern Europe – or for that matter Western Europe – today is therefore not necessarily to be taken as the refutation of the socialist utopia, still less of utopia *tout court*. Utopia has to be dissociated from its putative embodiment in various practices. There is plenty for it to do other than write party manifestos or 'recipes for the cookshops of tomorrow' (Marx's slighting but misapplied comment on utopias).

It can satirize and criticize; it can clarify standards and expectations; it can conduct thought-experiments, to try out new possible arrangements of social life; it can pick out and project hopeful trends, reworking them in a picture of future society that draws us on by the force of its imaginative realization. By its very extremism and one-sidedness, by the force and simplicity of its message, it can not only 'refurbish values and renew their impact on society' but it can also inject new values into the life of the community.[20] It can keep alive the 'principle of hope'.[21] It can serve as 'an imaginative reminder of the nature of historical change', by insisting, 'as a matter of general principle, that temporarily and locally incredible changes can and do happen'.[22] And it can contribute to that change by 'the education of desire'. It can open the way to aspiration because utopia can 'teach desire to desire, to desire better, to desire more, and above all to desire in a different way'.[23] Such a striving may, in utopia's most general effect, be open ended, the desire simply for something radically other. But utopia can also direct us to concrete, specific forms of the future. It can be, as Wells claimed, a form of sociology, 'knowledge rendered imaginatively', where the focus is on all the attempts, past, present and in an imagined future, to realize the harmonious 'Social Idea' in human civilization.[24]

There is, in short, no end to the uses of utopia.[25] It is a kind of thinking that has attracted philosophers, poets, political theorists, novelists, sociologists, scientists, theologians, architects, town planners, and statesmen. Almost as many intellectual disciplines have interested themselves in it for the purposes of study. Moreover its forms and functions have varied considerably over time. It was used in one way by moralists and political theorists in treatises concerned with the early impact of modern commerce and modern science; in another way by realist novelists exploring the problems of the new industrial society; and in still another way by science fiction writers responding to the social and psychological conditions of advanced industrial and post-industrial society. At various times too, and in different ways, it has given to social theory a heightened sense of social possibilities.

No simple, single strand of utopianism can therefore be privileged – whether for purposes of defence or attack. But this applies particularly to the contemporary enemies of utopia. It is they who have been busily engaged in conflating the varieties of utopia into a single uniform pattern. Often indeed utopianism is simply equated with Marxism. It is by constructing a type or model of 'the utopian mentality', or some such composite, that the anti-utopians have been able to launch their sharpest attacks. Such a mentality, it is claimed, must lead to tyranny and terror. In the face of this disingenuous procedure it may not be much use to point out that blaming, say, the socialist utopia for Stalinism is like blaming Christianity for the Inquisition.

The future of utopia

It is undeniable that in our own century it is the anti-utopian current that has been strongest. No great utopia has been written that has commanded the attention of the educated public in the manner of the utopias of Bellamy, Morris and Wells at the close of the last century. The texts which have been publicly debated have been in the main anti-utopias: *Brave New World*, *Darkness at Noon*, *Nineteen Eighty-Four*.

The anti-utopia of course pays tribute to utopia: the form, if not the content. Its imaginative portrait of a perfected society – a society that is a perfect nightmare – maintains in being the utopian way of doing things. Utopia may even – in principle at least – receive a fresh impetus from the challenge of the anti-utopia. It is forced to cast off the 'facile optimism' that some have seen as marking its later phases.[26] It is led to interrogate its own meaning and function in an age which seems to feel that it has realized at least some of the features of the modern utopia.

Moreover, the anti-utopia usefully highlights the persistent problem of how we read a utopia; what we take it to be. For Morris, Bellamy's *Looking Backward* was an anti-utopia. Huxley also read an anti-utopian meaning in Wells's utopian novel *Men Like Gods*. But Huxley's own *Brave New World* has been taken as a utopia by some contemporary hedonists; and Huxley himself deftly wrested utopia out of anti-utopia by putting the techniques of *Brave New World* to utopian purposes in *Island*. A little earlier the behavioural psychologist B. F. Skinner had done much the same thing in *Walden*

Two – a utopia which many outraged contemporaries read as a diabolical anti-utopia. Utopia and anti-utopia are mirror images of each other. Each can affect readers, even the same reader, in different ways at different times. William Morris once said that 'the only safe way of reading a utopia is to consider it as the expression of the temperament of its author'.[27] That is very good advice; but it leaves out the problem of the temperament of the reader.

Still, however we read the anti-utopia, it remains true that the literary utopia has had to struggle to survive for the best part of this century. The problem is not one of quantity. More utopias have probably been written in the last hundred years than in any previous century. This is a consequence largely of the growth of mass publishing, and of the development especially of the popular genre of science fiction. Some utopias of distinction have been written, as we shall see; but the majority are run of the mill science fiction stories in which the utopian setting is used as a vaguely evocative selling point by author and publisher.[28]

Things have been somewhat better for utopian social theory. In the mid-century the Marxist philosopher Ernst Bloch produced his passionate (and multi-volumed) plea for the reinstatement of utopia within Marxism, and generally for the recognition of the importance of utopia as an expression of the vital 'principle of hope' in human culture.[29] Other thinkers on the Left have also deplored Marxism's traditional hostility to utopianism and have sought to incorporate a utopian dimension in their thinking. Prominent among these are the 'Freudo-Marxists' such as Wilhelm Reich and Herbert Marcuse.[30] Jurgen Habermas, too, has offered something approaching a utopian model of social relations in his account of the 'ideal speech situation', the requisite conditions for rational communicative discourse between free and equal individuals.[31] And there has been Edward Thompson's magnificent reassessment of William Morris, from which he concludes that orthodox Marxism's disdain for Morris has involved

> the whole problem of the subordination of the imaginative utopian faculties within the later Marxist tradition: its lack of a moral self-consciousness or even a vocabulary of desire, its inability to project any images of the future, or even its tendency to fall back in lieu of these upon the Utilitarian's earthly paradise – the maximisation of economic growth.[32]

This urging of utopia on social theory has had some impact but, it is fair to say, not much. Part of the reason is its isolation from the mainstream socialist movement. Opposition to utopianism dies hard among socialists – despite, and in denial of, socialism's own origins in utopia. Since the rehabilitation of utopia has been most systematically attempted within the Marxist tradition, its marginality there and within the broader socialist movement has also meant that it has had relatively little influence within contemporary social theory at large.

Social movements are not, despite Mannheim's attempt to link them, essential to utopia. A sociology of utopias might make some rough correlations between times of particular stress or conflict within society and the appearance of some important utopias. This might work, for instance, for early seventeenth- and late nineteenth-century Europe. But in reality the whole of western history since the sixteenth century has been an epoch of crisis – just as the production of utopias has been well nigh continuous over the period, with some fluctuations. It is impossible to establish with any useful degree of precision a causal connection between the appearance of any utopia and its social context. At best we might discover social reasons for the reception (or otherwise) of particular utopias, and their usefulness to particular social movements. The enthusiastic adoption of Bellamy's *Looking Backward* by American Populists in the late nineteenth century is a good example of this.

But in a period in which utopia is, for whatever reason, weak or marginal, social movements can play some part in sustaining the utopian impulse and perhaps even stimulating a revival. Social movements need utopias even though they may not be the direct cause of them. They may therefore welcome whatever signs of utopian endeavour they find and seek to promote it as a valuable aid to the accomplishment of their goals. Certainly as we approach the end of the twentieth century the most vital currents of utopianism are to be found within the newer social movements that have arisen in response to the novel problems of late industrial society.

Chief among these is contemporary feminism. The recent phase of the feminist movement owes much of its driving force to the entry of women into the world of work in unprecedented numbers. New problems have arisen – for relations between men and women, the rearing of children, the arrangement of household work – which have given rise to a movement for interpreting and adjusting to the changes. The cultural expressions of the movement have been notable for their depth and intensity. These have included feminist plays, poetry, painting and music. They have also included feminist novels. Among these is a flourishing new genre of feminist utopias.

It was perhaps inevitable that women should take to utopia. Where else would they be free and equal? No known society in history has allowed them material or symbolic equality with men. Even in past utopias their situation has remained firmly subordinate to that of the men.[33] One of the earliest feminist utopias was indeed a spirited response to the portrayal of women in Edward Bellamy's hugely popular *Looking Backward*. Charlotte Perkins Gilman, American feminist, socialist and herself a member of the Nationalist movement inspired by Bellamy's book, felt the need to redress the balance so far as women were concerned. Drawing upon L. H. Morgan's work on primitive societies, her utopia *Herland* (1915) pictured a gentle matriarchal society in which men had been got rid of at an earlier date and women gave birth in an ecstatic act of parthenogenesis.

Gilman's example seems to have been infectious. Among more recent feminist utopias, the utopian society of Whileaway in Joanna Russ's *The Female Man* (1975) also gets on happily without men; while in Sally Gearhart's *The Wanderground* (1980), men are masters in their mechanized cities but in the countryside they are helpless in the face of women who have established all-female communities and have developed the powers of telepathy, telekinesis and even flight. Men are present, as equals, in Marge Piercy's *Woman on the Edge of Time* (1976); but her future society has borrowed *Brave New World* techniques of laboratory reproduction, thereby not merely freeing women from childbirth but allowing men to experience the joys and cares of motherhood along with the women ('we all became mothers. Every child has three').

The energy that has inspired these visions has also inspired their opposite: the feminist anti-utopia. In Margaret Atwood's *The Handmaid's Tale* (1986) women are enslaved to men, either as decorative spouses or as simple breeding machines. The antiutopia, here as in general, tends to take the form of an intensification and projection of currently existing patterns. Hence the feminist utopia often contains an explicit anti-utopia to highlight the present position of women. *The Female Man* plays with four alternative futures for women, at least two of which are dystopias of sexual inequality and degradation. *Woman on the Edge of Time* also includes a glimpse of an alternative future: a paranoid, power-mad world of massive inequality and exploitation, in which the women, continually remodelled by cosmetic surgery, exist simply as paid whores for the men. Ursula Le Guin's *The Dispossessed* (1974) contrasts an egalitarian utopia with an anti-utopia that closely mimics the reality of present day Western society. Women in utopia are the equal of men in politics, work, marriage, and scholarship; in anti-utopia their energy is consumed in competitive striving for the favours of wealthy and powerful men.

The Dispossessed is not just a feminist utopia; it is, perhaps even more, an ecotopia, an ecological utopia. So too are most feminist utopias, going back as far as *Herland*.[34] Male domination is often linked in these utopias to the exploitative and destructive uses of science and technology. Feminism and ecology are therefore often to be found conjoined in the same utopian works and for much the same reasons. For just as utopia has proved a creative form to the feminist movement in imagining futures for women, in trying out possible worlds, so too it has been stimulated by the requirements of the ecology movement for themes and images of an ecologically balanced and harmonious world.

Ernest Callenbach's *Ecotopia* (1975) appears to have named the form; but, as with the feminist utopia, the essence of the ecological utopia was presented much earlier, in William Morris's *News from Nowhere* (1890). Morris was the first to confront the juggernaut of industrialism not with nostalgic rejection nor technological socialism but with a humanized and aestheticized socialism that blended the best of Romanticism and Marxism. The utopian society of *News from Nowhere* is politically decentralized and environmentally and socially balanced. Town and country complement instead of contradicting each other. Production is for need and pleasure, not for profit, thus allowing the elimination of most of the apparatus of mass production and large-scale technology. Work is organized to be a source of pleasure and fulfilment; even the most humdrum household tasks are shown to be capable of being arranged according to this principle. Throughout beauty is taken to be the cardinal standard of society: beauty of things built, of the countryside worked, of goods produced, of dress worn, of the very appearance of the people. The beauty of the objects mirrors the beauty of the execution – the physical skill, creative thought and imagination – that goes into their making.

Here is an industrialism not rejected out of hand but strictly curbed, reorganized and redirected according to new goals of harmonious development and aesthetic enjoyment. Material growth is limited because its ceaseless expansion has brutalized the mass of the population and devastated the natural order. The relation between nature and society has had to be renegotiated. Old Hammond summarizes the change that has come about:

> England was once a country of clearings amongst the woods and wastes, with a few towns interspersed, which were fortresses for the feudal army, markets for the folk, gathering places for the craftsmen. It then became a country of huge and foul workshops and fouler gambling dens, surrounded by an ill-kept, poverty-stricken farm, pillaged by the masters of the workshops. It is now a garden, where nothing is wasted and nothing is spoilt, with the necessary dwellings, sheds, and workshops scattered up and down the country, all trim and neat and pretty.[35]

Unlike the feminist utopia, the ecotopia has never regained the heights it reached in its first expression. The rediscovery and reassessment of *News from Nowhere* has had to serve as a major point of reference in the current phase. Aldous Huxley's *Island* (1962), a marrying of Buddhist philosophy and Western science, can be taken as marking the opening of that phase. But it remained for some time an isolated example. The ecological movement developed strongly in the 1960s and 1970s but it seemed unwilling to cast its ideas in the form of utopia. Its main literary expression was to be found in science fiction. Frank Herbert's *Dune* (1965) was one of the best, with its portrait of the desert people, the Fremen, mastering by ecological understanding an arid and inhospitable environment. Overpopulation and ecological catastrophe were the themes of John Brunner's *Stand on Zanzibar* (1969) and *The Sheep Look up* (1972). And there were writers of fantasy, such as Russell Hoban, John Christopher and Richard Adams, who pitted nature against a mechanized society in an almost mystical affirmation of the former.[36] Such works recalled W. H. Hudson's primitivist utopia, *A Crystal Age* (1887). But unlike Hudson's book, none of these cases of science fiction or fantasy present full-fledged utopias, though an ecotopian vision is implicit in most of them.

It was though from science fiction that there appeared the best of the recent ecotopias, Ursula Le Guin's *The Dispossessed*. A complex work – originally subtitled 'An Ambiguous Utopia' – Le Guin presents a detailed picture of a decentralized, egalitarian society forced by its circumstances to accommodate to a harsh environment, and discovering in the process new ethical and social principles ('Excess is excrement', etc.). This is an open-ended, 'critical' utopia, but utopia it nevertheless is. Elsewhere in her work, as in *The Left Hand of Darkness* (1969) and *The Eye of the Heron* (1978), Le Guin has powerfully developed ecological ideas though without inscribing them in a formal utopia.[37] Her most ambitious effort so far is *Always Coming Home* (1986). A compilation rather than a conventional novel, this work gives a comprehensive account of a future people, the Kesh, who have established the most complete symbiosis with their natural environment. They relate to other animal species and to mountains, forests and lakes as to each other, in a unified cosmology. Le Guin shows great ingenuity in presenting their lives, culture and customs. But since the presentation aims more at a metaphorical evocation than a realistic description of the social order, it lacks, from the point of view of the ecotopia, the force of *The Dispossessed*.

Ecological ideas have indeed so far found their most powerful expression in utopian social theory rather than the literary ecotopia. The first stirrings of the movement in the 1960s and 1970s gave us Theodore Roszak's *Where the Wasteland Ends* (1972), E. F. Schumacher's *Small is Beautiful* (1973), and a succession of books by Ivan Illich (*De-Schooling Society*, 1971, etc.). Later, the impact of the new microtechnology on the world of work added a new urgency to thinking about the future. Traditional socialist concerns about the organization of production and the role of workers within it came to be linked to a wider ecological perspective. Red became Green.

In works such as André Gorz's *Farewell to the Working Class* (1982) and *Paths to Paradise* (1985), and in Rudolf Bahro's *From Red to Green* (1984) and *Building the Green Movement* (1986), the call has come for the abandonment of traditional attitudes to work and to the whole industrial imperative of economic growth. It was not, as Marx had claimed, that 'the realm of freedom' would be built upon and beyond 'the realm of necessity'. 'Necessity' itself had to be rethought: what was needed for a sustainable social life that was not grounded on inequality and exploitation but which at the same time did not depend upon the rape of other peoples and the natural

environment in the fulfilment of this goal. If abundance or a sur-
plus was seen as a requirement of freedom, then perhaps such
freedom was deceptive: a temporary breathing space for some at
the cost of deprivation for others, now and in the future. Far from
being beyond necessity, freedom might consist in a new recognition and understanding of it, and the reorganization of its sphere
along ecological lines.[38]

As we approach the end of the second millennium – and not just
because of the millennial sentiments this may arouse – we must
expect the new strivings and new strains of industrial society to require new pictures of the future. The feminist and ecological
movements are the first clear signs of a movement to a post-
industrial society, whatever its ultimate form. Other indications
are the changing nature of work and the vertiginous fluctuations in
the rates of employment and unemployment. Much of this is the
result of the emergence of a truly global society and a new international division of labour. Any account of the future that ignores
these developments will be worthless. But by the same token their
very novelty and urgency call for ways to help us to put them in
perspective and to guide our choices for the future.

What role will there be for utopia in this? As great as at any time
in its history, it should be clear. The weakness of utopian invention
for much of this century should not be taken as grounds for assum-
ing its inevitable or permanent demise. There were reasons, in the
history of our times, for doubting progress and for distrusting the
power of reason to reshape the world. So too there are now
reasons, at a different point in that history, for urging and ex-
pecting a renewal of utopia. This is not so much a matter of optimism or pessimism as of the magnitude of the problems facing us
and – more to the point – of the new possibilities for their resolution. At any time of great possibilities, hopes and fears mingle in
about equal proportions.

'Future histories' and other wide-ranging explorations of future
time are one helpful way of reflecting on those possibilities. They
attempt a systematic construction of a likely future world, drawing
on what they perceive to be the dominant developments of the
present time.[39] But by their forms they are obliged to be fair to all
the cross-currents and contradictions of the world as it is. Future
histories mix these in various more or less plausible ways, and may
or may not show them in a hopeful light. But their main purpose is

to assess and extrapolate current trends, not to favour some out of any sense of a desired future.

It is precisely this element of desire that is utopia's contribution. Utopia builds upon existing reality but is not imprisoned by it. It is formally forbidden to be some neutral, 'scientific' reflection of reality. It wishes to oppose some trends and to favour others, to throw its weight on the side of a desirable as well as a possible future. It is incurably partisan. Much of what is happening now is carried by powerful forces which, if left to their own motives and momentum, could build a hell rather than a heaven on earth. Utopia opposes as well as proposes. Its pictures of a fulfilled and happy humanity are premised on the rejection of some social impulses and the elevation of others. It is through this wilful suppression, by not showing certain things from our own world, that it negates their persistence into the future. Things need not continue as they are. Out of this defiance, set in a context that proposes an alternative, comes the desire for change and the hope that it may be possible. 'Once the inevitabilities are challenged, we begin gathering our resources for a journey of hope.'[40]

Utopia confronts reality not with a measured assessment of the possibilities of change but with the demand for change. This is the way the world should be. It refuses to accept current definitions of the possible because it knows these to be part of the reality that it seeks to change. In its guise as utopia, by the very force of its imaginative presentation, it energizes reality, infusing it, as Paul Tillich has said, with 'the power of the new'.[41] To some this has always appeared an abandonment rather to illusion and wish-fulfilment, to irresponsible fantasy in the face of 'the real world'. But there are different ways of grasping reality.

> What we call illusions are often, in truth, a wider vision of past and present realities – a willing movement of a man's soul with the larger sweep of the world's forces – a movement towards a more assured end than the chances of a single life.[42]

Wilde was right: 'A map of the world that does not include Utopia is not worth even glancing at.'

Notes

Chapter 1

1 More's book was published in Latin at Louvain (Belgium) in 1516. 'Utopia' was therefore strictly speaking a purely Latin word until Ralph Robinson's English translation of 1551. More's newly minted Latin word *utopia* was a conflation of various terms, on the late Greek model commonly used for scientific words: *ou* – not; *eu* – good or well; *topos* – a place; *-ia*, a suffix connoting region.

2 Thomas More, *Utopia* (and *A Dialogue of Comfort*), translated R. Robinson (London: Dent and Sons, Everyman Library, 1962), p. 15. Vespucci's account of his voyages was published in 1507.

3 R. Ames, *Citizen Thomas More and his Utopia* (Princeton, NJ: Princeton University Press, 1949), p. 8.

4 For a good critical review of interpretations, see Q. Skinner, 'More's *Utopia*', *Past and Present*, No. 38 (1967), pp. 153–68. See also Skinner, 'Sir Thomas More's *Utopia* and the Language of Renaissance Humanism', in A. Pagden, ed., *The Languages of Political Theory in Early-Modern Europe* (Cambridge: Cambridge University Press, 1987), pp. 123–58; J. H. Hexter, 'The Utopian Vision: Thomas More. *Utopia* and its Historical Milieux' in J. H. Hexter, *The Vision of Politics on the Eve of the Reformation: More, Machiavelli, and Seyssel* (London: Allen Lane, 1973), pp. 19–149.

5 More, *Utopia*, p. 135.

6 H. G. Wells, *A Modern Utopia* (Lincoln, NB: University of Nebraska Press, 1967), p. 6.

7 For some helpful discussion of this, see J. C. Davis, *Utopia and the Ideal Society: A Study of English Utopian Writing 1516–1700* (Cambridge: Cambridge University Press, 1983), pp. 1–40.

8 Conveniently reprinted, along with many others of a like kind, in Arthur O. Lovejoy and George Boas, *Primitivism and Related Ideas in Antiquity* (Baltimore, MD: Johns Hopkins University Press, 1935),

pp. 23–102. See also J. Z. Smith, 'Golden Age' in M. Eliade, ed., *The Encyclopaedia of Religion* (New York and London: Macmillan, 1987), Vol. 6, pp. 69–73. Here as well as in several of the following notes articles in this encyclopaedia are referred to as providing a convenient summary of recent scholarship as well as good bibliographies.

9 Quoted in R. Heinberg, *Memories and Visions of Paradise: Exploring the Universal Myth of the Golden Age* (Los Angeles: Jeremy P. Tarcher, 1989), p. 50. See also P.-E. Dumont, 'Primitivism in Indian Literature' in Lovejoy and Boas, *Primitivism and Related Ideas in Antiquity*, pp. 433–46. For other Eastern versions of the Golden Age see J. Chesneaux, 'Egalitarian and Utopian Traditions in the East', *Diogenes*, Vol. 62 (1968), pp. 76–102.

10 See Heinberg, *Memories and Visions of Paradise*, pp. 115–29; also M. Eliade, *The Myth of the Eternal Return, Or, Cosmos and History* (Princeton, NJ: Princeton University Press, 1971) and *Myth and Reality* (New York: Harper Colophon, 1975).

11 See G. Boas, 'Earthly Paradises' in *Essays on Primitivism and Related Ideas in the Middle Ages* (New York: Octagon Books, 1978), pp. 154–74; and generally on Paradise in Christianity and other cultures, see H. R. Patch, *The Other World According to Descriptions in Medieval Literature* (Cambridge, MA: Harvard University Press, 1950); M. Eliade, 'Paradise and Utopia' in F. E. Manuel, ed., *Utopias and Utopian Thought* (London: Souvenir Press, 1973), pp. 260–80; H. B. Partin, 'Paradise' in Eliade, *The Encyclopaedia of Religion*, Vol. 11, pp. 184–9.

12 Reprinted in a modernized form, in A. L. Morton, *The English Utopia* (London: Lawrence and Wishart, 1969), pp 279–85; see pp. 15–45 on Cockaygne more generally; and R. C. Elliott, *The Shape of Utopia: Studies in a Literary Genre* (Chicago: Chicago University Press, 1970), pp. 3–24.

13 On Jewish Messianism, see G. Scholem, 'Toward an Understanding of the Messianic Idea in Judaism' in *The Messianic Idea in Judaism, And Other Essays On Jewish Spirituality* (London: Allen and Unwin, 1971), pp. 1-36; R. J. Zwi Werblowsky, 'Jewish Messianism' in Eliade, ed., *The Encyclopaedia of Religion*, Vol. 9, pp. 472–7.

14 For a good critical discussion of the immense literature on millenarianism, see H. Schwartz, 'Millenarianism' in Eliade, ed., *The Encyclopaedia of Religion*, Vol. 9, pp. 521–32. See also S. Thrupp, ed., *Millennial Dreams in Action* (New York: Schocken Books, 1970); T. Olson, *Millennialism, Utopianism, and Progress* (Toronto: Toronto University Press, 1982), Part I.

15 See D. S. Crow, 'Islamic Messianism', in Eliade, *The Encyclopaedia of Religion*, Vol. 9, pp. 477–81.

16 See R. Shek, 'Chinese Millenarian Movements', in Eliade, *The*

Encyclopaedia of Religion, Vol. 9, pp. 532–6; Chesneaux, 'Egalitarian and Utopian Traditions in the East'; J. Needham, 'Social Devolution and Revolution: Ta Thung and Thai Phing' in R. Porter and M. Teich, eds, *Revolution in History* (Cambridge: Cambridge University Press, 1986), pp. 61–73.

17 L. Mumford, 'Utopia, the City and the Machine', in Manuel, ed., *Utopias and Utopian Thought*, p. 13. On the religious functions of early cities, see N. D. Fustel de Coulanges, *The Ancient City* (New York: Doubleday Anchor, n.d: first published in French in 1864).

18 See M. Tafuri, *Architecture and Utopia* (Cambridge, MA: MIT Press, 1979); H. Rosenau, *The Ideal City: Its Architectural Evolution in Europe* (London: Methuen, 1983); R. Fishman, 'Utopia in Three Dimensions: The Ideal City and the Origins of Modern Design' in P. Alexander and R. Gill, eds, *Utopias* (London: Duckworth, 1984), pp. 95–107, and *Urban Utopias in the Twentieth Century* (New York: Basic Books, 1977).

19 F. E. Manuel and F. P. Manuel, *Utopian Thought in the Western World* (Cambridge, MA: Harvard University Press, 1979), p. 94.

Chapter 2

1 Plato, *Timaeus*, in *Timaeus* and *Critias*, translated by Desmond Lee (Harmondsworth: Penguin Books, 1977), p. 39. The story is briefly summarized in the *Timaeus* and given at greater length in the (unfinished) *Critias*.

2 *Critias*, p. 145.

3 *Timaeus*, p. 36.

4 *Timaeus*, p. 38.

5 For the influence of the myth of Atlantis, see J. Bramwell, *Lost Atlantis: An Essay on the Atlantic Myth in Literature and Philosophy* (London: Cobden-Sanderson, 1937). He estimates that there have been over 5,000 books dealing with the lost continent. One of the best known is that by the American utopian writer I. Donnelly, *Antediluvian World* (1882).

6 *Timaeus*, p. 31.

7 The Utopian poem is printed in the Everyman edition of More's *Utopia*, p. 140.

8 This is the more modernized translation in *The Yale Edition of the Complete Works of St Thomas More*, Vol. 4: *Utopia*, Edward Surtz and J. H. Hexter, eds, (New Haven and London: Yale University Press, 1965), p. 107.

9 *Utopia*, (Everyman edition), p. 53.

10 Letter to Peter Giles, *Utopia* (Yale edition), p. 251.

11 See D. Lodge, 'Utopia and Criticism' *Encounter*, Vol. 32 (1969), pp. 65–75. Cf. N. Frye: 'Utopian thought is imaginative, with its roots in

literature . . . We have to see it as a species of the constructive literary imagination . . .' 'Varieties of Literary Utopias' in Manuel, *Utopias and Utopian Thought*, pp. 31–2.

12 For the inclusion of utopia in science fiction see D. Suvin, *Metamorphoses of Science Fiction: On the Poetics and History of a Literary Genre* (New Haven and London: Yale University Press, 1979), Part 1.

13 Lodge, 'Utopia and Criticism', p. 70.

14 On the close relation of utopia to satire, see Elliott, *The Shape of Utopia*, pp. 3–24.

15 See further on the anti-utopia, K. Kumar, *Utopia and Anti-Utopia in Modern Times* (Oxford and New York: Basil Blackwell, 1987), pp. 99–130.

16 See e.g. G. Negley and J. M. Patrick, *The Quest for Utopia: An Anthology of Imaginary Societies* (New York: Henry Schuman, 1952), p. 3. In her admirable survey, *Journey through Utopia* (London: Freedom Press, 1982), Marie Louise Berneri also – with the exception of Plato's *Republic* – deals almost exclusively with the literary utopia.

17 Manuel and Manuel, *Utopian Thought in the Western World*, p. 2. They take this expression from Sir Philip Sidney's definition of poetry, as 'a speaking picture, with this end, to teach and delight.' Sidney expressly mentions More's *Utopia* as 'poetic' in this sense. *A Defence of Poetry* (1595), ed. J. van Dorsten (Oxford: Oxford University Press, 1966), pp. 25, 33.

18 J. C. Davis, *Utopia and the Ideal Society: A Study of English Utopian Writing 1516–1700* (Cambridge: Cambridge University Press, 1983), p. 17; see also B. Goodwin and K. Taylor, *The Politics of Utopia: A Study in Theory and Practice* (London: Hutchinson, 1982), p. 27.

19 As does Frank Manuel in his introduction to *Utopias and Utopian Thought*, p. vii.

20 This theme, wider of course than simply the utopian tradition, is splendidly traced over the course of western intellectual history by J. Passmore, *The Perfectibility of Man* (London: Duckworth, 1972).

21 All the works mentioned in these two paragraphs are included by the Manuels in their encyclopaedic survey, *Utopian Thought in the Western World*. See also, for a similarly wide-ranging itemization of the utopian tradition, Goodwin and Taylor, *The Politics of Utopia*, p. 16.

22 See, e.g. Passmore, *The Perfectibility of Man*, p. 159.

23 B. de Jouvenel, 'Utopia for Practical Purposes' in Manuel, *Utopias and Utopian Thought*, p. 221.

24 Ibid., p. 223.

25 Karl Mannheim can speak for a host of commentators: 'It was Plato who furnished, notably in his *Republic*, the general model to which all later utopian fictions have been heavily indebted.' 'Utopia' in E. R. A.

Seligman and A. Johnson, eds, *The Encyclopaedia of the Social Sciences*, Vol. 15, (New York: Macmillan 1934), p. 200.

26 See the literature cited in notes 9–16, Chapter 1.

27 See J. Chesneaux, 'Egalitarian and Utopian Traditions in the East' *Diogenes*, Vol. 62 (1968) pp. 76–102. Chesneaux also claims a utopian tradition for the Buddhist countries of South-east Asia, especially Burma, Ceylon, Laos, Thailand, and Cambodia. But it is clear that he uses the term 'utopian' very loosely.

28 For a good brief account, together with many references, see J. Needham, 'Social devolution and revolution: *Ta Thung* and *Thai Phing*', in R. Porter and M. Teich, eds, *Revolution in History* (Cambridge: Cambridge University Press, 1986), pp. 61–73. See also Needham's *Science and Civilization in China*, Vol. 2: *History of Scientific Thought* (Cambridge: Cambridge University Press, 1956).

29 Needham, 'Social devolution and revolution', p. 68. He does not, however, call this utopianism.

30 There is an abridged English translation by L. G. Thompson, *Ta Thung Shu: The One-World Philosophy of Khang Yu-Wei* (London: Faber and Faber, 1958).

31 Despite the implication of the title of the article by F. Graus, 'Social Utopias in the Middle Ages', *Past and Present*, No. 38 (1967), pp. 3–19. What Graus discusses, as he himself admits, are not utopias but village Cockaygnes and popular myths of the Golden Age. The absence of utopia in the Middle Ages is generally accepted: see, e.g. J. O. Hertzler, *The History of Utopian Thought* (New York: Cooper Square Publishers, 1965), p. 121; Olson, *Millennialism, Utopianism and Progress*, p. 159.

32 Augustine's view as summarized by M. Eliav-Feldon, *Realistic Utopias: The Ideal Imaginary Societies of the Renaissance 1516–1630* (Oxford: Clarendon Press, 1982), p. 5.

33 R. W. Chambers, *Thomas More* (London: Jonathan Cape, 1935), p. 128.

34 M. I. Finley, 'Utopianism Ancient and Modern' in K. H. Wolff and Barrington Moore Jr, eds, *The Critical Spirit: Essays in Honor of Herbert Marcuse* (Boston: Beacon Press, 1967), p. 6. Darko Suvin also calls utopia a 'this-worldly other world': *Metamorphoses of Science Fiction*, p. 42. For the contrary view, that utopia is closely related to Christian thought, see Manuel and Manuel, *Utopian Thought in the Western World*, *passim*; see also K. Löwith, *Meaning in History* (Chicago: Chicago University Press, 1949). For a general discussion, see Krishan Kumar, *Religion and Utopia* (Canterbury: Centre for the Study of Religion and Society, University of Kent, 1985).

35 Olson, *Millennialism, Utopianism, and Progress*, pp. 144. 157.

36 See *Diodorus Siculus*, translated by C. H. Oldfather, The Loeb

Classical Library (Cambridge, MA: Harvard University Press, 1979), Book 2, pp. 55–60; Book 5, pp. 41–6. We should note that More consciously distances his *Utopia* from these fairy tales:'. . . as for monsters, because they be no news, of them we were nothing inquisitive. For nothing is more easy to be found than be barking Scyllas, ravening Celaenos, and Laestrygons, devourers of people, and suchlike great and incredible monsters. But to find citizens ruled by good and wholesome laws, that is an exceeding rare and hard thing.' *Utopia* (Everyman edition), p. 18.

37 Finley, 'Utopianism Ancient and Modern', pp. 10–11.

38 Plato, *The Republic*, translated by B. Jowett (New York: Vintage Books, nd), p. 59 (Book II, 369). See also on Plato's purpose in the *Republic*, P. Alexander, 'Grimm's Utopia: Motives and Justification', in Alexander and Gill, *Utopias*, pp. 31–42; Frye, 'Varieties of Literary Utopias', pp. 32–4.

39 *The Republic*, p. 360 (Book IX, 592). Cf. also pp. 201–2 (Book V, 472).

40 *The Republic*, p. 284 (Book VII, 536).

41 Plato, *The Seventh Letter*, in *Phaedrus and Letters VII and VIII*, translated by Walter Hamilton (Harmondsworth: Penguin Books, 1973), pp. 136, 138.

Chapter 3

1 Arthur Koestler, autobiographical essay in Richard Crossman, ed., *The God That Failed* (New York: Bantam Books, 1965), p. 12. George Orwell's remark is in his essay, 'Arthur Koestler', in *The Collected Essays, Journalism and Letters of George Orwell*, 4 vols, edited S. Orwell and I. Angus (Harmondsworth: Penguin Books, 1970), Vol. 3, p. 274. The Manuels also speak of 'the mythic sub-stratum of modern utopian thought' (*Utopian Thought in the Western World*, p. 64). See also Negley and Patrick, *The Quest for Utopia*, p. 252; G. Kateb, *Utopia and Its Enemies* (New York: Schocken Books, 1972), p. 9.

2 E.g. T. Kenyon, 'Utopia in Reality: "Ideal" Societies in Social and Political Theory', *History of Political Thought*, Vol. 3 (1982) pp. 123–55.

3 Davis, *Utopia and the Ideal Society*, p. 5.

4 Ibid., p. 6.

5 Olson, *Millennialism, Utopianism, and Progress*, p. 143. Cf. also J. Shklar: 'Utopia is nowhere, not only geographically but historically as well. It exists neither in the past nor in the future.' 'The Political Theory of Utopia: From Melancholy to Nostalgia', in Manuel, *Utopias and Utopian Thought*, p. 104.

6 Q. Skinner, 'Meaning and Understanding in the History of Ideas',

History and Theory, Vol. 8 (1969), pp. 38–9. See also, for a similar view, J. Dunn, 'The Identity of the History of Ideas', *Philosophy*, Vol. 43 (1968), pp. 85–116.

7 Although it is odd, and I think highly misleading, to suggest as Davis does that Skinner's approach can be *equated* with the belief in the existence of traditions of thought (*Utopia and the Ideal Society*, p. 2). Skinner's scepticism regarding that comes out in his statement that to attempt any history that might demonstrate such a tradition for a given concept would be 'an almost absurdly ambitious enterprise.' ('Meaning and Understanding', p. 39).

8 For the parallel example of the concept of revolution, see K. Kumar, 'Revolution, Past and Present' in C. Davies, ed., *The Meaning of Contemporary Revolution* (London: Routledge, forthcoming).

9 For some, necessarily incomplete, evidence of this see the listings in R. W. Gibson and J. Max Patrick, 'Utopias and Dystopias, 1500–1750', in R. W. Gibson, ed., *St. Thomas More: A Preliminary Bibliography of the Works and Moreana to the Year 1750* (New Haven: Yale University Press, 1961); A. B. Samaan, 'Utopias and Utopian Novels: 1516–1949: A Preliminary Bibilography' *Moreana*, Vols 31/32 (1971); L. T. Sargent, *British and American Utopian Literature 1516–1985: An Annotated Chronological Bibliography* (New York: Garland Publishing, 1988): G. Negley, *Utopian Literature: A Bibliography with a Supplementary Listing of Works Influential in Utopian Thought* (Lawrence, KS: The Regents Press, 1977); Negley and Patrick, *Quest for Utopia*, pp. 19–22; R. Gerber, *Utopian Fantasy: A Study of English Utopian Fiction Since the End of the Nineteenth Century* (London: Routledge and Kegan Paul, 1955), Appendix, pp. 143–60. The various histories and commentaries, e.g. the Manuels, *Utopian Thought in the Western World*, make much the same point.

10 J. H. Hexter, 'The Utopian Vision: Thomas More. *Utopia* and Its Historical Milieux' in *The Vision of Politics on the Eve of the Reformation: More, Machiavelli, and Seyssel* (London: Allen Lane, 1973), p. 118.

11 L. Mumford, 'Utopia, the City and the Machine' in Manuel, *Utopias and Utopian Thought*, p. 9. See also Finley, 'Utopianism Ancient and Modern', pp. 14–16.

12 Aristotle, *The Politics*, translated by Ernest Barker (Oxford: Clarendon Press, 1952), pp. 52–4 (Book II. v).

13 Plato, *The Republic*, translated by B. Jowett, p. 127 (Book III, 416).

14 *The Republic*, pp. 189–90 (Book V, 464).

15 *The Republic*, p. 127 (Book III, 417).

16 For a comparison of the communism of Plato and More, see E. Barker, *Greek Political Theory: Plato and his Predecessors* (London: Methuen, 1957), pp. 206–38, 385–8; J. H. Hexter, *More's Utopia: The Biography*

of an Idea (Princeton, NJ: Princeton University Press, 1952), pp. 83–5 and 'The Utopian Vision: Thomas More', pp. 88–9, 120–7; Olson, *Millennialism, Utopianism and Progress*, pp. 152–3.

17 J. H. Hexter, 'The Predatory and the Utopian Vision: Machiavelli and More. The Loom of Language and the Fabric of Imperatives: The Case of *Il Principe* and *Utopia*', in *The Vision of Politics on the Eve of the Reformation*, pp. 179–203.

18 A persuasive formulation here is I. Wallerstein, *The Modern World System*, 2 vols (New York and London: Academic Press, 1974 and 1980).

19 See P. B. Gove, *The Imaginary Voyage in Prose Fiction* (New York: Columbia University Press, 1941).

20 See especially Charles Webster's study of the Samuel Hartlib circle, the central driving force in promoting the 'new philosophy' of Bacon in mid-seventeenth-century England: *The Great Instauration: Science, Medicine, and Reform 1626–1660* (London: Duckworth, 1975). The same point is more generally made by K. Thomas, *Religion and the Decline of Magic* (Harmondsworth: Penguin Books, 1973).

21 See J. C. Davis, 'Science and Utopia: The History of a Dilemma' in E. Mendelsohn and H. Nowotny, eds, *Nineteen Eighty-Four: Science between Utopia and Dystopia* (Dordrecht: D. Reidel, 1984).

22 E. L. Tuveson, *Millennium and Utopia: A Study in the Background of the Idea of Progress* (New York: Harper Torchbooks, 1964).

23 On the Pansophias of the seventeenth-century proponents of science, see Manuel and Manuel, *Utopian Thought in the Western World*, pp. 205–331.

24 F. E. Manuel, 'Toward a Psychological History of Utopias' in Manuel, *Utopias and Utopian Thought*, pp. 72–9; See also for the utopias of the sixteenth to eighteenth centuries, E. Hansot, *Perfection and Progress: Two Modes of Utopian Thought* (Cambridge, MA and London: MIT Press, 1974).

25 See M. Poster, *The Utopian Thought of Restif de la Bretonne* (New York: New York University Press, 1971).

26 For utopias of the Enlightenment, see Berneri, *Journey Through Utopia*, pp. 174–206; A. Cioranescu, *L'Avenir du Passé: Utopie et Littérature* (Paris: Gallimard, 1972), pp. 156–89. For Foigny's utopia, see the English abridgement in Negley and Patrick, *Quest for Utopia*, pp. 401–19; Diderot's utopia is similarly abridged in F. E. Manuel and F. P. Manuel eds, *French Utopias: An Anthology of Ideal Societies* (New York: Schocken Books, 1971), pp. 149–66; this collection also contains many of the lesser known French utopias.

27 Although not in itself a sexual utopia, most of the elements of it are contained in Wayland Young, *Eros Denied* (London: Weidenfeld and Nicolson, 1967). See also, on the 'Freudo-Marxists', P. Robinson, *The*

Freudian Left (New York: Harper & Row, 1969).

28 On the 'planetary novel' see M. H. Nicolson, *Voyages to the Moon* (New York: Macmillan, 1948); Suvin, *Metamorphoses of Science Fiction*, pp. 97–114.

29 L. S. Mercier, *L'An 2440*, translated and abridged in Negley and Patrick, *Quest for Utopia*, p. 488. On the rise of the 'tale of the future' see I. F. Clarke, *The Pattern of Expectation 1644–2001* (New York: Basic Books, 1979), pp. 15–61. There is a good brief survey of the idea of progress in S. Pollard, *The Idea of Progress* (Harmondsworth: Penguin Books, 1971); see also Olson, *Millennialism, Utopianism and Progress*, pp. 219–62.

30 Quoted in F. E. Manuel, *The New World of Henri Saint-Simon* (Notre Dame, IN: University of Notre Dame Press, 1963), p. 160.

31 See for an example, C. Brinton, 'Utopia and Democracy' in Manuel, *Utopias and Utopian Thought*, pp. 50–68.

32 N. Frye, 'Varieties of Literary Utopias' in Manuel, *Utopias and Utopian Thought*, p. 36. See also P. Alexander, 'Grimm's Utopia: Motives and Justification' in Alexander and Gill, *Utopias*.

33 See J. Shklar, 'The Political Theory of Utopia' and *After Utopia: The Decline of Political Faith* (Princeton, NJ: Princeton University Press, 1957).

34 See Kumar, *Utopia and Anti-Utopia in Modern Times*, pp. 49–65; Z. Bauman, *Socialism: The Active Utopia* (London: Allen and Unwin, 1976); V. Geoghegan, *Utopianism and Marxism* (London and New York: Methuen, 1987).

Chapter 4

1 For More, Bellamy and the Incas, see A. E. Morgan, *Nowhere Was Somewhere: How History Makes Utopias and How Utopias Make History* (Chapel Hill: The University of North Carolina Press, 1946) and *Edward Bellamy* (Philadelphia: Porcupine Press, 1974), pp. 301 ff.

2 F. E. Manuel, *The Prophets of Paris* (New York: Harper Torchbooks, 1965), pp. 154–5.

3 See S. Yeo, 'A New Life: The Religion of Socialism in Britain, 1883–1896', *History Workshop Journal*, No. 4 (1977), pp. 5–56.

4 See Kumar, *Utopia and Anti-Utopia in Modern Times*, pp. 149–58.

5 See C. Hill, 'The Norman Yoke', in *Puritanism and Revolution* (Harmondsworth: Penguin Books, 1986), pp. 58–125; R. Paulson, *Representations of Revolution (1789–1820)* (New Haven and London: Yale University Press, 1983), pp. 1–36; P. Meier, *William Morris*, 2 vols (Hassocks: Harvester Press, 1978), Vol. I, pp. 94–164.

6 Kumar, *Utopia and Anti-Utopia in Modern Times*, Chapters 7 and 8.

7 G. Orwell, *Nineteen Eighty-Four* (Harmondsworth: Penguin Books, 1954), pp. 212–13.

8 Plato's account is in his *Seventh Letter* (see Chapter 2, note 41).

9 C. L. Sanford, *The Quest for Paradise: Europe and the American Moral Imagination* (Urbana: University of Illinois Press, 1961), pp. 56–73; H. M. Jones, *O Strange New World* (London: Chatto & Windus, 1965).

10 C. H. Johnson, *Utopian Communism in France: Cabet and the Icarians 1839–51* (Ithaca, NY: Cornell University Press, 1974). For the Icarian communities in America, see note 22, below.

11 Manuel and Manuel, *Utopian Thought in the Western World*, p. 254.

12 For a brief account, see A. R. Hall, *The Scientific Revolution 1500–1800*, 2nd edn. (London: Longmans, 1962), pp. 192–5; and cf. Harry Levin, 'The Great Good Place' *New York Review of Books*, 6 March 1980, p. 48.

13 D. Hume, 'Idea of a Perfect Commonwealth' (1754), in *Essays: Moral, Political and Literary*, ed. E. F. Miller (Indianopolis: Liberty Classics, 1987), p. 514.

14 See H. F. Russel Smith, *Harrington and his Oceana: A Study of a Seventeenth Century Utopia and Its Influence in America* (Cambridge: Cambridge University Press, 1914); J. G. A. Pocock, *The Machiavellian Moment* (Princeton, NJ: Princeton University Press, 1975), Part 3.

15 For Sieyès's constitution of 1799, see the 'Introduction' to *What is the Third Estate?*, translated M. Blondel (London: Pall Mall Press, 1963), pp. 22–4.

16 See K. Kinkade, *A Walden Two Experiment: The First Five Years of Twin Oaks Community* (New York: William Morrow, 1973).

17 For further development see K. Kumar 'Utopian Thought and Communal Practice: Robert Owen and the Owenite Communities', *Theory and Society*, Vol. 19 (1990), pp. 1–35.

18 Manuel and Manuel, *Utopian Thought in the Western World*, p. 9.

19 Y. Friedman, *Utopies Réalisables* (Paris: Union Générale d'Editions, 1975).

20 B. Goodwin and K. Taylor, *The Politics of Utopia: A Study in Theory and Practice* (London: Hutchinson, 1982), pp. 218–22.

21 A. Elzinga and A. Jamison, 'Making Dreams Come True – An Essay on the Role of Practical Utopias in Science' in Mendelsohn and Nowotny, *Nineteen Eighty-Four*, p. 160.

22 For the American communities, see M. Holloway, *Heavens on Earth: Utopian Communities in America 1680–1880* (New York: Dover Publications, 1966); A. E. Bestor Jr, *Backwoods Utopias: The Sectarian and Owenite Phases of Communitarian Socialism in America, 1663–1829* (Philadelphia, PA: University of Philadelphia Press, 1950) and 'Patent-Office Models of the Good Society', *American Historical*

Review, Vol. 58 (1953), pp. 505–26; Y. Oved, *Two Hundred Years of American Communes* (New Brunswick, NJ: Transaction Books, 1988).

23 Quoted in J. F. C. Harrison, *Robert Owen and the Owenites in Britain and America: The Quest for a New Moral World* (London: Routledge and Kegan Paul, 1969), p. 145.

24 Quoted in E. P. Thompson, *The Making of the English Working Class* (London: Gollancz, 1963), p. 789.

25 J. H. Noyes, *History of American Socialisms* (Philadelphia: J. B. Lippincott, 1870), p. 670. Cf. also Bestor, *Backwoods Utopias*, p. 59.

26 Quoted in L. S. Feuer, 'The Influence of the American Communist Colonies on Engels and Marx', *Western Political Quarterly*, Vol. 19 (1966), p. 459.

27 Bestor, *Backwoods Utopias*, p. 38.

28 See on the British communities, D. Hardy, *Alternative Communities in Nineteenth Century England* (London: Longman, 1979); W. H. G. Armytage, *Heavens Below:Utopian Experiments in England 1560–1960* (London: Routledge and Kegan Paul, 1961); J. Marsh, *Back to the Land: The Pastoral Impulse in Victorian England from 1880–1914* (London: Quartet Books, 1982).

29 Harrison, *Robert Owen and the Owenites*, p. 175; cf. Hardy, *Alternative Communities*, p. 211. For the causes of failure, see R. M. Kanter, *Commitment and Community: Communes and Utopias in Sociological Perspective* (Cambridge, MA: Harvard University Press, 1972); C. J. Erasmus, *In Search of the Common Good: Utopian Experiments Past and Future* (New York: Free Press, 1977).

30 Quoted in R. S. Fogarty, *Dictionary of American Communal and Utopian History* (Westport, CT: Greenwood Press, 1980), p. xiv.

31 Correspondent to *The Labour Annual 1900*, quoted in Hardy, *Alternative Communities*, p. 215.

32 Sargent, *British and American Utopian Literature*, p.x.

33 See e.g. Kateb, *Utopia and Its Enemies*, pp. 12–13.

34 A. Huxley, 'Ozymandias', in *Adonis and the Alphabet* (London: Chatto & Windus, 1956), p. 100.

35 See Bestor, *Backwoods Utopias*, pp. 133–59; G. B. Lockwood, *The New Harmony Movement* (New York: D. Appleton and Co., 1905), pp. 314–77.

36 See B. Taylor, *Eve and the New Jerusalem: Socialism and Feminism in the Nineteenth Century* (New York: Pantheon Books, 1983).

37 See A. Fein, 'Fourierism in Nineteenth-Century America: A Social and Environmental Perspective' in M. Allain, ed., *France and North America: Utopias and Utopians* (Baton Rouge, LA: University of South Louisiana, 1978), pp. 133–48.

38 For communes in the second half of the twentieth century see, from an

extensive literature, P. Abrams and A. McCulloch, *Communes, Sociology and Society* (Cambridge: Cambridge University Press, 1976); A. Rigby, *Alternative Realities: A Study of Communes and their Members* (London: Routledge and Kegan Paul, 1974): K. Melville, *Communes in the Counter-Culture* (New York: William Morrow, 1972); R. Houriet, *Getting Back Together* (New York: Coward, McCann and Geoghegan, 1971).

39 M. Buber, *Paths in Utopia* (Boston: Beacon Press, 1958), p. 99; for Weber, see ibid., p. 128.

40 For one example, see the splendid study by R. Jenkyns, *The Victorians and Ancient Greece* (Oxford: Basil Blackwell, 1980).

41 Not to be confused with the 'world government' or 'world state' utopia, which has been quite common – especially in the writings of H. G. Wells and his followers. See W. W. Wagar, *H. G. Wells and the World State* (New Haven: Yale University Press, 1961).

42 G. W. F. Hegel, *The Philosophy of History*, translated J. Sibree (New York: Dover Publications, 1956), p. 85.

43 Engels quoted in D. Bell, *Marxian Socialism in the United States* (Princeton, NJ: Princeton University Press, 1967), p. 3.

44 Quoted in Lockwood, *The New Harmony Movement*, p. 70.

45 J. Baudrillard, *America*, translated C. Turner (London: Verso, 1989), p. 77.

46 F. Fanon, *The Wretched of the Earth*, translated C. Farrington (Harmondsworth: Penguin Books, 1967), p.252.

47 See R. Crossman, ed., *The God That Failed* (New York: Bantam Books, 1965); D. Caute, *The Fellow Travellers* (London: Weidenfeld and Nicolson, 1973).

48 Crossman, *The God That Failed*, p. 176.

49 N. Bobbio, 'The Upturned Utopia', *New Left Review*, No. 177 (1989), p. 37.

Chapter 5

1 The description is in Suvin, *Metamorphoses of Science Fiction*, p. 100n.

2 Negley, *Utopian Literature*, p. xxii.

3 See Chapter 2 above, p. 31.

4 See J. H. Hexter, 'The Utopian Vision', pp. 126–7; also 'The Predatory and the Utopian Vision', pp. 179–203.

5 Thomas More, *Utopia*, eds, G. M. Logan and R. M. Adams (Cambridge: Cambridge University Press, 1989), p. 39.

6 *Utopia*, p. 37.

7 de Jouvenel, 'Utopia for Practical Purposes', p. 220.

8 Karl Popper, 'Utopia and Violence' in *Conjectures and Refutations: The Growth of Scientific Knowledge* (London: Routledge and Kegan

Paul, 1965), pp. 358–63. For similar objections, see F. A. Hayek, *The Road to Serfdom* (London: Routledge and Kegan Paul, 1944); M. Oakeshott, 'Rationalism in Politics' in *Rationalism in Politics and Other Essays* (London: Methuen, 1962); J. Talmon, 'Utopianism and Politics' in G. Kateb, ed., *Utopia* (New York: Atherton Press, 1971); M. Lasky, *Utopia and Revolution* (London: Macmillan, 1976). From a sociological perspective there is Ralf Dahrendorf, 'Out of Utopia: Toward a Reorientation of Sociological Analysis' in *Essays in the Theory of Society* (London: Routledge and Kegan Paul, 1968). For good critical discussions of the anti-utopian arguments see Kateb, *Utopia and Its Enemies*; B. Goodwin, 'Utopia Defended Against the Liberals', *Political Studies*, Vol. 28, pp. 384–400 (1980). Kateb observes that 'the most inclusive book' for the expression of anti-utopian feeling, especially as regards utopian means, is Karl Popper's *The Open Society and Its Enemies* (first edition, London: Routledge and Kegan Paul, 1945); Nietzsche is seen as providing 'the most inclusive critique' of utopian ends: *Utopia and Its Enemies*, p. 19.

9 L. Kolakowski, 'The Death of Utopia Reconsidered' in S. M. McMurrin, ed., *The Tanner Lectures on Human Values 4 (1983)* (Cambridge: Cambridge University Press, 1983), p. 238.

10 On the grounds for such a reasoned pessimism today, see Joe Bailey, *Pessimism* (London and New York: Routledge, 1988).

11 Karl Mannheim, 'Utopia'; see also Mannheim, *Ideology and Utopia* (London: Routledge and Kegan Paul, 1960), pp. 173–90.

12 N. Berdyaev, 'Democracy, Socialism and Theocracy', in *The End of Time*, translated by D. Attwater (London: Sheed, 1933), p. 188. I have altered the translation somewhat. That this view sums up the essential anti-utopian objection is argued in Kateb, *Utopia and Its Enemies*, pp. 13–14; see also G., Woodcock, 'Utopias in the Negative' *Sewanee Review*, Vol. 64 (1956), p. 82; E. Weber, 'The Anti-Utopia of the Twentieth Century', *South Atlantic Quarterly*, Vol. 58 (1959), pp. 440–1.

13 N. Mandelstam, BBC *Radio 3*, 18 January 1981.

14 Kolakowski, 'The Death of Utopia Reconsidered', pp. 240, 242.

15 See, e.g. N. Bobbio, 'The Upturned Utopia', *New Left Review* No. 177 (1989), pp. 37–9; and, from a different angle, F. Fukuyama, 'The End of History?' *The National Interest*, Summer 1989, pp. 3–18. For months in late 1989 and early 1990 the press in Western Europe and North America resounded with pronouncements of 'the death of utopia'. See, e.g., P. Jenkins, 'The Death of a Modern Creed', *The Independent*, 6 February 1990. For the death of utopia in Eastern Europe, see W. Lepenies, 'Melancholy of Utopian Shadows', *Times Higher Education Supplement*, 12 January 1990; J. Lloyd, 'Letter from Prague', *Samizdat*, No. 8 (1990) p. 26.

16 Oscar Wilde, 'The Soul of Man Under Socialism' (1891), in *De Profundis and Other Writings*, edited Hesketh Pearson (Harmondsworth: Penguin Books, 1973), p. 34.

17 See Gerber, *Utopian Fantasy*, pp. 131–2.

18 Z. Bauman, *Socialism: The Active Utopia* (London: Allen and Unwin, 1976), p. 47; see also Bauman, 'From Pillars to Post', *Marxism Today*, February (1990), pp. 20–25.

19 Ibid., p. 20.

20 H. J. N. Horsburgh, 'The Relevance of the Utopian', *Ethics*, Vol. 67 (1957), pp. 136–7.

21 Ernest Bloch, *The Principle of Hope* (Oxford: Basil Blackwell, 1986).

22 Raymond Williams, *The Year 2000* (New York: Pantheon Books, 1983), p. 13; cf. Geoghegan, *Utopianism and Marxism*, p. 2.

23 M. Absensour, quoted in E. P. Thompson, *William Morris: Romantic to Revolutionary* (London: Merlin Press, 1977), p. 791.

24 H. G. Wells, 'The So-Called Science of Sociology', in *An Englishman Looks at the World* (London: Cassell and Co., 1914), pp. 192–206; see also K. Kumar, 'Wells and the So-Called Science of Sociology', in P. Parrinder and C. Rolfe, eds, *Wells Under Revision* (London and Toronto: Associated University Presses, 1990), pp. 192–217.

25 For some other uses, see F. Bloch-Lainé, 'The Utility of Utopias for Reformers' in Manuel, *Utopias and Utopian Thought*; Goodwin and Taylor, *The Politics of Utopia*, pp. 207–25; A. Hacker, 'In Defense of Utopia' in P. E. Richter, ed., *Utopias: Social Ideals and Communal Experiments* (Boston: Holbrook Press, 1971); T. Kitwood, '"Utopia" and "Science" in the Anticipation of Social Change', *Alternative Futures*, Summer (1978), pp. 24–46.

26 Gerber, *Utopian Fantasy*, p. 132.

27 W. Morris, 'Looking Backward', *The Commonweal*, 22 June 1889; in M. Morris, *William Morris: Artist, Writer, Socialist*, 2 vols (Oxford: Basil Blackwell, 1936), Vol. 2, p. 502.

28 See for an example from a popular and respected science fiction writer, F. Pohl's *Jem* (New York: Bantam Books, 1980). On science fiction and utopia, see Suvin, *Metamorphoses of Science Fiction*, *passim*; R. Williams, 'Utopia and Science Fiction' in *Problems in Materialism and Culture* (London: Verso, 1980); T. Moylan, *Demand the Impossible: Science Fiction and the Utopian Imagination* (New York and London: Methuen, 1986); P. Parrinder, *Science Fiction: Its Criticism and Teaching* (London and New York: Methuen, 1980), pp. 76–82.

29 E. Bloch, *The Principle of Hope* (Oxford: Basil Blackwell, 1986).

30 See Kumar, *Utopia and Anti-Utopia in Modern Times*, pp. 393–401.

31 J. Habermas, *The Theory of Communicative Action*, 2 vols (Boston: Beacon Press, 1984–86).

32 Thompson, *Morris*, p. 792. And cf. P. Anderson: 'All creative socialist

thought is likely to possess a utopian dimension.' 'Utopias' in *Arguments within English Marxism* (London: New Left Books, 1980), p. 175n. He cites as a good recent example R. Bahro's *The Alternative in Eastern Europe* (London: New Left Books, 1978).

33 See L. T. Sargent, 'Women in Utopia', *Comparative Literature Studies*, Vol. 10 (1973), pp. 302–16; E. H. Baruch, '"A Natural and Necessary Monster"': Women in Utopia' *Alternative Futures: The Journal of Utopian Studies*, Vol. 26 (1979), pp. 29–48.

34 For discussion of the feminist utopia, see C. Pearson, 'Women's Fantasies and Feminist Utopias' *Frontiers: A Journal of Women's Studies*, Vol. 2 (1977), pp. 50–61; A. Mellor, 'On Feminist Utopias' *Women's Studies*, Vol. 9 (1982), pp. 241–62; T. Moylan, *Demand the Impossible: Science Fiction and the Utopian Imagination* (New York and London: Methuen, 1986); F. Bartkowski, *Feminist Utopias* (Lincoln: University of Nebraska Press, 1989); special issue, 'Women and the Future', *Alternative Futures*, Vol. 4 (1981).

35 W. Morris, *News from Nowhere* (1890) in *Three Works by William Morris* (London: Lawrence and Wishart, 1973), p. 254.

36 See A. Swinfen, *In Defence of Fantasy: A Study of the Genre in English and American Literature since 1945* (London: Routledge and Kegan Paul, 1984), pp. 190–229.

37 For a discussion of Le Guin's work, see J. D. Olander and M. H. Greenberg, eds, *Ursula Le Guin* (New York: Taplinger, 1979); Moylan, *Demand the Impossible*, pp. 91–120.

38 On these thinkers, see B. Frankel, *The Post-Industrial Utopians* (Cambridge: Polity Press, 1987).

39 See e.g. N. Macrae, *The 2024 Report: A Concise History of the Future 1974–2024* (London: Sidgwick and Jackson, 1984); B. Stableford and D. Langford, *The Third Millennium: A History of the World AD 2000–3000* (London: Paladin Books, 1988).

40 Williams, *The Year 2000*, p. 268.

41 P. Tillich, quoted in J. R. Stumme, *Socialism in Theological Perspective: A Study of Paul Tillich 1918–33* (Butte, MT: Scholars Press, 1978), p. 188. See also P. Tillich, 'Critique and Justification of Utopia' in Manuel, *Utopias and Utopian Thought*, pp. 298–99.

42 G. Eliot, *Felix Holt, the Radical* (Harmondsworth: Penguin Books, 1972), p. 276.

Bibliography

Abrams, P. and McCulloch, A., *Communes, Sociology and Society* (Cambridge: Cambridge University Press, 1976).

Alexander, P., 'Grimm's Utopia: Motives and Justification', in P. Alexander and R. Gill, eds, *Utopias* (London: Duckworth, 1984).

Alexander, P. and Gill, R., eds, *Utopias* (London: Duckworth, 1984).

Allain, M., ed., *France and North America: Utopias and Utopians* (Baton Rouge, LA: University of Southern Louisiana, Center for Louisiana Studies, 1978).

Anderson, P., 'Utopias' in P. Anderson, *Arguments Within English Marxism* (London: New Left Books, 1980).

Armytage, W. H. G., *Heavens Below: Utopian Experiments in England 1560–1960* (London: Routledge and Kegan Paul, 1961).

Bailey, J., *Pessimism* (London and New York: Routledge, 1988).

Bartkowski, F., *Feminist Utopias* (Lincoln, NB: University of Nebraska Press, 1989).

Baruch, E. H., '"A Natural and Necessary Monster": Women in Utopia', *Alternative Futures: The Journal of Utopian Studies*, Vol. 26 (1979).

Bauman, Z., *Socialism: The Active Utopia* (London: Allen and Unwin, 1976).

Bauman, Z., 'From Pillars to Post', *Marxism Today*, February (1990).

Berneri, M. L., *Journey Through Utopia* (London: Freedom Press, 1982).

Bestor, Arthur E. Jr, *Backwoods Utopias: The Sectarian and Owenite Phases of Communitarian Socialism in America, 1663–1829* (Philadelphia PA: University of Philadelphia Press, 1950).

Bloch, E., *The Principle of Hope*, (Oxford: Basil Blackwell, 1986, 3 vols).

Bloch-Lainé, F., 'The Utility of Utopias for Reformers' in F. E. Manuel, ed., *Utopias and Utopian Thought* (London: Souvenir Press, 1973).

Boas, G., *Essays on Primitivism and Related Ideas in the Middle Ages* (New York: Octagon Books, 1978).

Bobbio, N., 'The Upturned Utopia', *New Left Review*, No. 177 (1989).

Bramwell, J. G., *Lost Atlantis: An Essay on the Atlantic Myth in Literature and Philosophy* (London: Cobden-Sanderson, 1937).

Brinton, C., 'Utopia and Democracy' in F. E. Manuel, ed., *Utopias and Utopian Thought* (London: Souvenir Press, 1973).

Buber, M., *Paths in Utopia* (Boston: Beacon Press, 1958).

Chesneaux, J., 'Egalitarian and Utopian Traditions in the East', *Diogenes*, Vol. 62 (1968).

Cioranescu, A., *L'Avenir du Passé: Utopie et Littérature* (Paris: Gallimard, 1972).

Clarke, I. F., *The Pattern of Expectation 1644–2001* (New York: Basic Books, 1979).

Dahrendorf, R., 'Out of Utopia: Toward a Reorientation of Sociological Analysis' in *Essays in the Theory of Society* (London: Routledge and Kegan Paul, 1968).

Davis, J. C., *Utopia and the Ideal Society: A Study of English Utopian Writing 1516–1700* (Cambridge: Cambridge University Press, 1983).

Davis, J. C., 'Science and Utopia: The History of a Dilemma' in E. Mendelsohn and H. Nowotny, eds, *Nineteen Eighty-Four: Science Between Utopia and Dystopia* (Dordrecht: D. Reidel, 1984).

Eliade, M., *The Myth of the Eternal Return, Or, Cosmos and History* (Princeton, NJ: Princeton University Press, 1971).

Eliade, M., *Myth and Reality* (New York: Harper Colophon, 1975).

Eliade, M., ed., *The Encyclopaedia of Religion* (New York and London: Macmillan, 1987, 16 vols).

Eliav-Feldon, M., *Realistic Utopias: The Ideal Imaginary Societies of the Renaissance 1516–1630* (Oxford: Clarendon Press, 1982).

Elliot, R. C., *The Shape of Utopia: Studies in a Literary Genre* (Chicago: Chicago University Press, 1970).

Elzinga, A. and Jamison, A., 'Making Dreams Come True – An Essay on the Role of Practical Utopias in Science' in E. Mendelsohn and H. Nowotny, eds, *Nineteen Eighty-Four* (Dordrecht: D. Reidel, 1984).

Erasmus, C., *In Search of the Common Good: Utopian Experiments Past and Future* (New York: Free Press, 1977).

Ferguson, J., *Utopias of the Classical World* (London: Thames and Hudson, 1975).

Finley, M. I., 'Utopianism Ancient and Modern' in K. H. Wolff and Barrington Moore Jr, eds, *The Critical Spirit: Essays in Honor of Herbert Marcuse* (Boston: Beacon Press, 1967).

Fishman, R., *Urban Utopias in the Twentieth Century: Ebenezer Howard, Frank Lloyd Wright and Le Corbusier* (New York: Basic Books, 1977).

Frankel, B., *The Post-Industrial Utopians* (Cambridge: Polity Press, 1987).

Friedman, Y., *Utopies Réalisables* (Paris: Union Générale d'Editions, 1975).

Frye, N., 'Varieties of Literary Utopias' in F. E. Manuel, ed., *Utopias and Utopian Thought* (London: Souvenir Press, 1973).

Fukuyama, F., 'The End of History?', *The National Interest*, Summer 1989.

Geoghegan, V., *Utopianism and Marxism* (London and New York: Methuen, 1987).

Gerber, R. *Utopian Fantasy: A Study of English Utopian Fiction Since the End of the Nineteenth Century* (London: Routledge and Kegan Paul, 1955).

Goodwin, B., 'Utopia Defended Against the Liberals', *Political Studies*, Vol. 28 (1980).

Goodwin, B. and Taylor, K., *The Politics of Utopia: A Study in Theory and Practice* (London: Hutchinson, 1982).

Gove, P. B., *The Imaginary Voyage in Prose Fiction, 1700–1800* (New York: Columbia University Press, 1941).

Hacker, A., 'In Defense of Utopia' in P. E. Richter, ed., *Utopias: Social Ideals and Communal Experiments* (Boston: Holbrook Press, 1971).

Hansot, E., *Perfection and Progress: Two Modes of Utopian Thought* (Cambridge, MA and London: MIT Press, 1974).

Hardy, D., *Alternative Communities in Nineteenth Century England* (London: Longman, 1979).

Harrison, J. F. C., *Robert Owen and the Owenites in Britain and America: The Quest for the New Moral World* (London: Routledge and Kegan Paul, 1969).

Hayek, F. A., *The Road to Serfdom* (London: Routledge and Kegan Paul, 1944).

Heinberg, R., *Memories and Visions of Paradise: Exploring the Universal Myth of the Golden Age* (Los Angeles, CA: Jeremy P. Tarcher, 1989).

Hertzler, J. O., *The History of Utopian Thought* (New York: Cooper Square Publishers, 1965).

Hexter, J. H., *The Vision of Politics on the Eve of the Reformation: More, Machiavelli and Seyssel* (London: Allen Lane, 1973).

Holloway, M., *Heavens on Earth: Utopian Communities In America 1680–1880* (New York: Dover Publications, 1966).

Horsburgh, H. J. N., 'The Relevance of the Utopian', *Ethics*, Vol. 67 (1957).

Houriet, R., *Getting Back Together* (New York: Coward, McCann and Geoghegan, 1971).

Jouvenel, B. de, 'Utopia for Practical Purposes' in F. E. Manuel, ed., *Utopias and Utopian Thought* (London: Souvenir Press, 1973).

Kanter, R. M., *Commitment and Community: Communes and Utopias in Sociological Perspective* (Cambridge MA: Harvard University Press, 1972).

Kateb, G., *Utopia and Its Enemies* (New York: Schocken Books, 1972).

Kenyon, T., 'Utopia in Reality: "Ideal" Societies in Social and Political Theory', *History of Political Thought*, Vol. 3 (1982).

Kitwood, T., '"Utopia" and "Science" in the Anticipation of Social Change', *Alternative Futures*, Summer (1978).

Kolakowski, L., 'The Death of Utopia Reconsidered' in S. M. McMurrin, ed., *The Tanner Lectures on Human Values IV (1983)* (Cambridge: Cambridge University Press, 1983).

Kumar, K., *Religion and Utopia* (Canterbury: Centre for the Study of Religion and Society, University of Kent, 1985).

Kumar, K., *Utopia and Anti-Utopia in Modern Times* (Oxford and New York: Basil Blackwell, 1987).

Kumar, K., 'Utopian Thought and Communal Practice: Robert Owen and the Owenite Communities', *Theory and Society*, Vol. 19, (1990).

Lasky, M., *Utopia and Revolution* (London: Macmillan, 1976).

Levin, H., 'The Great Good Place', *New York Review of Books*, 6 March 1980.

Lodge, D., 'Utopia and Criticism', *Encounter*, Vol. 32 (1969).

Lovejoy, A. O. and Boas, G., *Primitivism and Related Ideas in Antiquity* (Baltimore, MD: Johns Hopkins University Press, 1935).

Löwith, K., *Meaning in History* (Chicago: Chicago University Press, 1949).

Mannheim, K., 'Utopia' in E. R. A. Seligman and A. Johnson, eds, *The Encyclopaedia of the Social Sciences*, Vol. 15 (New York: Macmillan, 1934).

Mannheim, K., *Ideology and Utopia* (London: Routledge and Kegan Paul, 1960).

Manuel, F. E., 'Toward a Psychological History of Utopias' in F. E. Manuel, ed., *Utopias and Utopian Thought* (London: Souvenir Press, 1973).

Manuel, Frank E., ed., *Utopias and Utopian Thought* (London: Souvenir Press, 1973).

Manuel, F. E. and Manuel, F. P., eds, *French Utopias: An Anthology of Ideal Societies* (New York: Schocken Books, 1971).

Manuel, F. E. and Manuel, F. P., *Utopian Thought in the Western World* (Cambridge, MA: Harvard University Press, 1979).

Marsh, J., *Back to the Land: The Pastoral Impulse in Victorian England from 1880–1914* (London: Quartet Books, 1982).

McCord, W., *Voyages to Utopia: Visions and Realities* (New York: Norton, 1990).

Mellor, A., 'On Feminist Utopias', *Women's Studies*, Vol. 9 (1982).

Melville, K., *Communes in the Counter-Culture* (New York: William Morrow, 1972).

Mendelsohn, E. and Nowotny, H., eds, *Nineteen Eighty-Four: Science Between Utopia and Dystopia* (Dordrecht: D. Reidel, 1984).

Morgan, A. E., *Nowhere was Somewhere: How History Makes Utopias and*

How Utopias Make History (Chapel Hill, NC: The University of North Carolina Press, 1946).

Morton, A. L., *The English Utopia* (London: Lawrence and Wishart, 1969).

Moylan, T., *Demand the Impossible: Science Fiction and the Utopian Imagination* (New York and London: Methuen, 1986).

Mumford, L., 'Utopia, the City and the Machine' in F. E. Manuel, ed., *Utopias and Utopian Thought* (London: Souvenir Press, 1973).

Negley, G., *Utopian Literature. A Bibliography with a Supplementary Listing of Works Influential in Utopian Thought* (Lawrence, KS: The Regents Press, 1977).

Negley, G., and Patrick, J. M., *The Quest for Utopia: An Anthology of Imaginary Societies* (New York: Henry Schuman, 1952).

Oakeshott, M., 'Rationalism in Politics' in *Rationalism in Politics and Other Essays* (London: Methuen, 1962).

Olson, T. *Millennialism, Utopianism, and Progress* (Toronto: Toronto University Press, 1982).

Oved, Y., *Two Hundred Years of American Communes* (New Brunswick, NJ: Transaction Books, 1988).

Parrinder, P., *Science Fiction: Its Critcism and Teaching* (London and New York: Methuen, 1980).

Passmore, J., *The Perfectibility of Man* (London: Duckworth, 1972).

Pearson, C., 'Women's Fantasies and Feminist Utopias', *Frontiers: A Journal of Women's Studies*, Vol. 2 (1977).

Pollard, S., *The Idea of Progress* (Harmondsworth: Penguin Books, 1971).

Popper, K., 'Utopia and Violence' in *Conjectures and Refutations: The Growth of Scientific Knowledge* (London: Routledge and Kegan Paul, 1965).

Richter, P. E., ed., *Utopias: Social Ideals and Communal Experiments* (Boston: Holbrook Press, 1971).

Rigby, A., *Alternative Realities: A Study of Communes and their Members* (London: Routledge and Kegan Paul, 1974).

Rosenau, H., *The Ideal City: Its Architectural Evolution in Europe* (London: Methuen, 1983).

Samaan, A. B., 'Utopias and Utopian Novels: 1516–1949: A Preliminary Bibliography', *Moreana*, Vol. 31/32 (1971).

Sargent, L. T., 'Women in Utopia', *Comparative Literature Studies*, Vol. 10 (1973).

Sargent, L. T., *British and American Utopian Literature 1516–1985: An Annotated Chronological Bibliography* (New York: Garland Publishing, 1988).

Shklar, J., 'The Political Theory of Utopia: From Melancholy to Nostalgia' in F. E. Manuel, ed., *Utopias and Utopian Thought* (London: Souvenir Press, 1973).

Shklar, J., *After Utopia: The Decline of Political Faith* (Princeton, NJ: Princeton University Press, 1957).

Suvin, D., *Metamorphoses of Science Fiction: On the Poetics and History of a Literary Genre* (New Haven and London: Yale University Press, 1979).

Swinfen, A., *In Defence of Fantasy: A Study of the Genre in English and American Literature Since 1945* (London: Routledge and Kegan Paul, 1984).

Tafuri M., *Architecture and Utopia* (Cambridge, MA: MIT Press, 1979).

Talmon, J., 'Utopianism and Politics' in G. Kateb, ed., *Utopia* (New York: Atherton Press, 1971).

Taylor, B., *Eve and the New Jerusalem: Socialism and Feminism in the Nineteenth Century* (New York: Pantheon Books, 1983).

Thrupp, S., ed., *Millennial Dreams in Action* (New York: Schocken Books, 1970).

Tillich, P., 'Critique and Justification of Utopia' in F. E. Manuel, ed., *Utopias and Utopian Thought* (London, Souvenir Press, 1973).

Tuveson, E. L., *Millennium and Utopia: A Study in the Background of the Idea of Progress* (New York: Harper Torchbooks, 1964).

Weber, E., 'The Anti-Utopia of the Twentieth Century', *South Atlantic Quarterly*, Vol. 58 (1959).

Williams, R., 'Utopia and Science Fiction' in *Problems in Materialism and Culture* (London: Verso, 1980).

Williams, R., *The Year 2000* (New York: Pantheon Books, 1983).

Woodcock, G., 'Utopias in the Negative', *Sewanee Review*, Vol. 64 (1956).

Index